Praise for Hank Moore

" **A**ny serious organization would do well to listen to this man. He speaks of genius, creativity, and plain common sense."

—George H.W. Bush,
former President of the United States

" **Y**our words of wisdom have reminded our members of those bigger issues which we sometimes overlook in the day-to-day performance of work."

—Thomas Gentry,
American Institute of Architects

The
Business
Tree

Growth Strategies and Tactics for Surviving and Thriving

HANK MOORE

CAREER
PRESS

Franklin Lakes, NJ

THE BUSINESS TREE
EDITED BY JODI BRANDON
TYPESET BY EILEEN MUNDON
Cover design by Rob Johnson/Johnson Design
Printed in the U.S.A. by Courier

To order this title, please call toll-free 1-800-CAREER-1 (NJ and Canada: 201-848-0310) to order using VISA or MasterCard, or for further information on books from Career Press.

CAREER
PRESS

The Career Press, Inc., 3 Tice Road, PO Box 687,
Franklin Lakes, NJ 07417
www.careerpress.com

Library of Congress Cataloging-in-Publication Data

Moore, Hank.
    The business tree : growth strategies and tactics for surviving and thriving /
  by Hank Moore.
        p. cm.
    Includes index.
    ISBN 978-1-60163-094-0
    1. Strategic planning. 2. Corporations--Growth. I. Title.

HD30.28.M6453 2010
658.4'06--dc22

                                                    2009040489

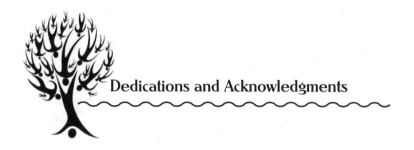

Dedications and Acknowledgments

Special dedications go to my wife (April), my sisters (Jane Moore Taylor and Julie Moore), and my grandchildren (Courtney Hamlyn, Henry Wilson, Austin Zepeda, Tad Hamlyn, Thomas Zepeda, Erin Hamlyn, AnnaMarie Zepeda, and Samantha Ponton).

Dedications go to other family members, including Sally Choate, Bill Garrett, Tina Mabe Hamlyn, Jesse Mueller, Larry Mueller, Lizzie Mueller, Chris Ponton, Tamra Ponton, Bill Taylor, Cindy Taylor, Deborah Taylor, Jon Taylor, Paige Taylor, John Zepeda, and Rebecka Zepeda.

Professional dedications and acknowledgments go to Jay Abraham, Peter Bijur, Dick Clark, Dave Conti, Heather Covault, Stephen Covey, W. Edwards Deming, Barry Diller, Lou Dobbs, Peter Drucker, Michael Eisner, Lyn Fisher, Mark French, Carl Glaw, Andrea Gold, Dr. Norman Hackerman, Michael Hick, Jan K. Jones, Carl Kasell, Herb Kelleher, Ben Love, Ed Madden, Dennis McQuistion, Bill Moyers, Robert Osborne, Dan Parsons, Tom Peters, Cactus Pryor, Bill Richardson, Anthony Robbins, Peter Sagal, Peter Senge, David L. Smith, Jacqueline Taylor, Rich Tiller, and John Willig.

Professional dedications and acknowledgments go to my colleagues in the Silver Fox Advisors: Bruce Anderson, Dr. Harlene Anderson, Gordon Arnold, Ed Bick, Tim Clay, Ginger Coleman, George Connelly, John Curtiss, Diana Dale, Ralph D'Onofrio, Jim Fish, Roger Flink, Tom Gillis, Noel Graubart, Jim Griffing, Marie Guillot, Sonny Harkins, Dick Hendee, Ken Jones, Howard London, Butch Madrazo, Herschel Maltz, Melvin Maltz, Jay Marks, Grace Martinez, Mark Miller, Phil Morabito, Joe Munisteri, John Ogren, Monte Pendleton, Rick Schissler, Bob Schwartz, Gerry Seay, Glen Shepard, Lane Sloan, Wayne Smithers, Bill Spitz, Dennis Stavinoha, Bill Stephens, Dan Steppe, Terry Stockham, Keith Thayer, Jack West, Bill Wheelock, Carl Wilson, and Tom Woehler.

Dedications and acknowledgments also to: Robert Battle, Cannon Robert Brooks, Jackie Broussard, Dr. Lee P. Brown, Tony Castiglie, Hector and Arleigh DeLeon, David Dickey, Dr. Ron Evans, Elroy Forbes, Dr. George Glass, Diane Gomez, Royce Heslep, Susan Hutsko, Dan Krohn, Rich Latimer, Torre Lee, Kent LeMonte, Mike Linares, Jim McKinley, David Melasky, Paul Muñoz, Carter and Eloise Rochelle, Lyle Ruybalid, Mike Scott, Jack and Jean Shabot, Bill and Joan Spitz, Ed Shane, Maggie Steber, James and Carolyn Todd, Les Venmore, Jose Villarreal, and Martha Wong.

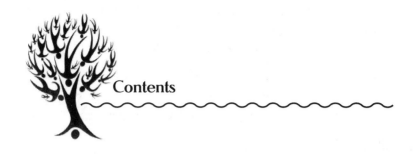

Contents

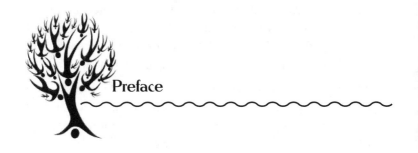

Preface

Business is at a most decisive crossroads. Corporate scandals and mistrust in business put all of us in the position of picking up the pieces and moving forward.

The rules have changed—always have and always will. A great many mosaics make up The Big Picture. Yet the wider perspective in business is rarely seen. Too many myopic niches dominate the view.

This book is about widening the scope much further. Whenever we review what made the business successful, we see that big-picture thinking took part in past times, before the micro mindsets took over.

The potential of organizations is a progressive journey from information to insight. Foolhardiness is all about being righteous about inconsequential things at the wrong times. People and organizations spend disproportionate amounts of time trying to behave like or look like someone else—or what they think others appear to be. Until one becomes one's own best role model, the futile trail will continue.

The chapters in this book are written in such a way as to be interpreted on several levels. Part common sense and part deep wisdom, they are intended to widen your focus and inspire the visionary that exists within you the reader.

When you and your company widen the scope and advocate strategic planning and visioning, I will have fulfilled my mentoring role. Futuristic ideas can and should become your ideas, mindset, and ethical business practice.

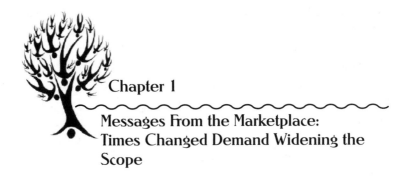

Chapter 1

Messages From the Marketplace:
Times Changed Demand Widening the
Scope

Times of crisis and economic downturn get people thinking differently about the conduct of business. Organizations
say that they need to re-evaluate and get back to basics, that
nothing is guaranteed. They realize that the old ways of doing
business will no longer work. They seek to better themselves
as professionals and to rethink the business models. Changing
times require new perspectives.

For some, these are stark new approaches. This is the reality in which the small business and entrepreneurial worlds have
always experienced. Welcome to the paradigms that many of
us have operated under for some time.

Accepting change as a positive guiding principle, one then
seeks to find, analyze, and apply fresh approaches toward addressing the old problems. For many, times of crisis mandate
that they think boldly and get used to doing business that way
henceforth.

This book is an exploration into the creativity, the opportunities, and the potential rewards of reflecting differently
upon business. Our intention and the experiences of many
companies who have followed the model presented here is

that organizations must now learn how to paint their own "big pictures" of business, rather than focusing upon certain niches. They benefit from change, while the non-change stagnates become additional casualties.

A gun without instructions on its safe use becomes a deadly weapon. Medication usage without diagnosis and treatment by a properly trained and skilled physician is also dangerous. Making financial investments without conducting research and developing a strategy will lead to economic crisis. Continuing to turn a deaf ear to the voices of reason and alternate opinions leads to the condition of hubris, which brings companies and societies down.

The purpose of this book is to offer enlightened insights into running a business. These are the kinds of insights that others before me did not have when they embarked upon careers. This is not the approach that is taught in business schools and really should be. As one who has seen, heard, and influenced good companies, my hope is to show the good organizations how to become much greater through a larger-scope focus, backed by the strategies to accomplish high goals.

I offer the voice of encouragement to the two youngest generations in the workforce. The objective is to help readers to avoid falling into the same traps that brought their elders' companies down before their times had come. This book includes many of the insights that the elder generations never had, never were taught, or couldn't see on the paths up the career ladder. I have seen many good companies go down in flames because management would not open up the focus any further or make the necessary changes before it was simply too late.

You could call this book the experiences and observations of a credible second opinion, sometimes a third or fourth one. I'm the one who comes in after businesses made the wrong turns or had the wrong consultants dispensing inappropriate advice. I'm the one who suggests that getting back to basics and rethinking where they've been and where they're going might be prudent.

Narratives are from my perspective as your business mentor. This body of wisdom reflects lessons from excellent mentors, teachers, and role models whom I had the pleasure of knowing. It is a book filled with the things that I was never taught in business school but learned in the real world.

Most people who have followed my work say that the ideas and insights are 90-percent common sense, and the creative ideas reflect the gemstones inside each company's goldmine. People always ask, "Why don't we hear this common-sense approach more often? Why do few look wide enough at business opportunities? Why don't ethics and best practices get portrayed as profitable business strategies? Why are the same niche perspectives always heard?"

My response is that business people are more wider-picture oriented than they might perceive or allow themselves to be. However, society is more inclined toward favoring certain niche perspectives.

Business is all too often lumped with finance. Economic advisors propose bailouts, whereas seasoned business advisors recommend marketplace corrections and corporate culture changes. Bean counters see business as mostly numbers. Trainers see a learning organization filled with classes of students, thus becoming a vendor commodity in the eyes of buyers. Marketers always look toward the next campaign and view business in terms of slogans and images. Process people see only the steps necessary to produce goods.

Every niche perspective figures into a big picture, but does not constitute the whole by itself. It is vital to view the relationship of all necessary components to each other and in support of a discernable whole.

> ## Key Messages to Recall and Apply Toward Your Business Future
>
> ➡ Understand the big picture.
>
> ➡ Benefit from change.
>
> ➡ Avoid false idols and facades.
>
> ➡ Remediate the high costs of band-aid surgery.
>
> ➡ Learn from the mistakes made by other companies.
>
> ➡ Plan and benchmark.
>
> ➡ Craft and sustain the vision.

I have learned that good businesses do not set out to go bad. They just don't set out with a delineated plan, backed with cohesive strategies to make the plan workable. Widening the scope and conducting meaningful planning are the only true routes toward surviving, thriving, and moving forward—when times are tough, when times are prosperous, and during every business cycle in between.

Yes, those who waited until they were in dire trouble to rethink and move in different directions could have attained those strategies much earlier. Exceptional lawyers, accountants, and other top business advisors all know that calling them sooner rather than later would have lessened the damages on the clients' ends.

Human beings are not perfect and don't do everything right on the front end. We learn more workable strategies through trial and error. Organizations full of human beings need the impetus to think new creative thoughts, without the judgment of past mistakes. Those who continue to make the same mistakes thus become the case studies from which good companies learn the next round of lessons.

That's the rationale for this book. It is predicated upon thinking more holistically about company operations. It poses a business landscape populated by new thoughts that address seemingly insurmountable problems. There is and always will be a fresh new panorama just ahead and ready to paint. The ways in which we build, nurture, and compost the landscape will reap the true and more continuing rewards.

The business climate ahead is tough and is filled with uncertainty, all of which translates into opportunities for those who are alert. Those others who believe that the old ways still work shall fall by the wayside. Innovation and the ability to fill new niches will signal the successful businesses of the future.

Take this quick test, as part of your strategic planning for the next two to five years. Ask yourself some questions:

DOES YOUR COMPANY HAVE a cohesive business plan, with results-oriented positioning and marketing objectives, updated every year?

WHAT IS THE NATURE of your business now, as compared to when you entered it? What has changed, and who are the new entrants?

WHICH MARKETPLACE FACTORS are within your grasp? Which are out of your control? Which factors do your competitors control? Which opportunities to overtake the competition are within your company's plan of action?

HOW WELL DOES the marketplace understand your organization and its value to the business bottom line? Are there misperceptions that need changing?

HOW MUCH HAS your company given back to the communities in which you do business? Is there an organized plan of reciprocation, with a business development design? Do you know who your stakeholders are and how they might benefit you by working more closely with them?

How well trained are your employees? Do they know, hold, and embrace the company vision? With some fine-tuning, how much could you multiply the effectiveness of your empowered workforce?

In an era of downsizing, cutbacks, and a reluctance to expand, there are four principles of growing a company:

1. Sell new customers. Without adding to the base, the business goes flat.

2. Cross-sell existing customers. Most customers are not fully aware of all the product-service lines that you offer. It's your obligation to inform buyers about all that you have to offer, facilitating their ability to make wise choices. A satisfied clientele is easier to see credibility in your company.

3. Create and market new products-services. Having one good mousetrap does not mean that the public will automatically beat a path to your door. One must be alert to the next trends, the newest products, and the next logical extension of his/her company in the marketplace.

4. Creatively partner in order to create additional marketplace opportunities. By combining disciplines, you can attract new business and pursue new, creative solutions for clients. Business can no longer do business as a bunch of lone rangers. (This concept will be discussed at length in Chapter 8.)

In order to tackle the challenges of the future, each company must assess its current position. One must presuppose that little or no strategic planning was previously done and then paint a fresh landscape.

Only 2 percent of the businesses in the world actually have functioning strategic plans. This means that 98 percent of all the companies in the world have no real strategic plan. They may have sales quotas or financial projections, but a collection of such memos does not constitute authentic strategic plans. Is it any wonder that so many businesses steer off course or never really make their journeys in the first place?

Research and "what if" scenario-building are what comprise the foundation for effective strategic planning. Company leaders must weigh all of the circumstances and situations in crafting plans. Then, they should formulate workable strategies. Always, we should measure the process and its results.

This book is about building successful strategies to navigate business in the new order. With turbulence and accelerated changes, the opportunities for survival and long-term success are quite varied.

Eighty-two percent of all the companies that exist are small and emerging businesses. Ninety-eight percent of all new business starts are small and emerging businesses. Seventy percent of all companies die in their first five years. Forty percent of those that do not plan will fail soon.

Ninety percent of firms are out of business by year 10. The four-year survival rate in the information sector is 38 percent. The four-year survival rate in education and health services sector is 55 percent. The average startup in education and health sector is 50 percent more likely than the average startup in the information sector to live four years. Forty percent of all start-up restaurants fail.

Forty-five percent of small business owners are children of small business owners. Eighty-three percent of all domestic companies have fewer than 20 employees. Only 7 percent of all companies have 100 or more employees.

The primary categories of small businesses are: retail, build a new mousetrap, clone other mousetraps, pursue a dream that was started elsewhere, transition company (nurturing to grow and then sell to someone else), investment company, and the providing of professional services.

I've talked with many entrepreneurs and founders of companies that rapidly grew from the seeds of ideas they had germinated. Most admitted enjoying the founding phase but lost interest shortly after giving birth. Over and over, they said, "When it stops being fun, I move on."

After the initial honeymoon, you speak with them and hear rumblings such as this: "It isn't supposed to be this hard. Whatever happened to the old days? This seems too much like running a business. I'm an idea person, and all this administrative stuff is a waste of my time. I'm ready to move on to the next challenge."

At this point, they expect the business to transition itself smoothly and still make the founders some money. They ask, "Are you the one who comes in here and looks after my interests?" I reply, "No. After the caretakers have come in and applied the wrong approaches to making something of your business, I'm the one who comes in afterward, cleans up after the 'band-aid surgery' was applied, and helps to restart the business again."

Full-scope business planning is much more effective on the front end, helping business owners avoid the costly pitfalls attached to their losing interest and abdicating to the wrong activities. When the "fun" ends, the hard work begins. It is crucial for principals of the small business to follow their dreams, develop a cohesive strategic plan, find an effective working style, match the actions to the corporate culture, and stay with the program sufficiently long enough to measure results.

Businesses usually stop growing because they have failed to make investments for future company success. Rather than plan to grow and follow the plan, they rationalize organizational setbacks, excuse poor service or quality, and avoid change, all the while denying the need for change and avoiding any planning. Too often, they rely upon what worked for them in the past, on buzzwords, and on incomplete strategies. We've all seen businesses in which a paralysis creeps in, keeping them from doing anything at all.

A growth plan or strategic plan is essential for any organization that intends to survive and thrive in today's rapidly changing business environment. Companies need to heed messages from the marketplace telling them of changing market conditions, new global business imperatives, new partnering concepts, recognition of new stakeholders, and other changes outside of their influence that may profoundly affect them.

Not only do they need to know where they are going, but they need the tools to assess continually their plans in response to what the market is telling them. I have advised many businesses in their journey to the next plateau, or toward recovery after a setback, or as they attempt to change course.

Time and time again, I have found that companies spend so much time correcting or reshaping small pieces of their business puzzle—reacting to immediate concerns and crises—that they neglect the long-term. The cost of such a piecemeal approach (I call it band-aid surgery) is high, costing up to six times the price of planning on the front end.

My remedy is an approach to planning using a proprietary model I call The Business Tree™. Following it forces management to take a holistic approach to looking at their business and the marketplace, and developing their plans for growth.

The number seven appears frequently in this book. There are seven major parts to the tree. Seven is also the number of progressions toward meaningful growth.

This book is all about creating and sustaining seven important business mindsets for your organization:

1. Look to craft innovative strategies to achieve steady, managed growth.

2. Analyze and fine-tune your product and process realignment. Collaborations are the most viable way to build sustainable business.

3. Human intelligence is the most important tool in your arsenal. You are in the credibility business. People are the company's most important resource and must be developed, rewarded, and empowered.

4. Professional development, performance reviews, ethics, values, accountabilities, and the court of public opinion all matter. All must be addressed in strategic planning.

5. Business is an honorable trust. Those who understand and utilize best practices will grow. Those who do not will fail.

6. Build a realistic and dynamic organization. The careful nurturing of your vision will yield results.

7. ~~Never stop thinking, planning, dreaming, and teaming.~~

The Business Tree is the centerpiece of this book, and, through it, readers will learn to strategize and plan with the entire business in view.

I have spent the last 20 years developing this model and overview philosophy of business. Most of the case studies in this book represent cases where this model, creative new thinking, and new approaches to the business resulted in successes.

I decided upon a tree as a business symbol because it's something that we see every day, in some form or other. The tree represents the organization as a whole. Each major branch then symbolizes a component or aspect of the company, including the core business, running the business, finance, people, business development, the organization's body of knowledge, and where it is headed.

In spite of most organizations' inability to plan, forward-thinking people really do want things to operate effectively.

They work toward goals, attend workshops, read books, and seek out the best advice of consultants. They get discouraged when top management cannot recognize the paths of improvement that they see or recommend. They feel stuck and realize that inertia has set into their company or that management has settled for the status quo.

The process of periodic review and evaluation can help remedy the situation. All too often, management is caught in the daily grind and unfortunately believes that strategic planning is a luxury. The folks in the executive suites need to be gently reminded of what visionaries they could truly become. The review process looks at nuggets of gold and makes good companies great. That's what senior management must believe and model for employees in the new order of business.

In this book, I challenge readers to realize their companies' hidden strengths. I have learned again and again that the best opportunities come through periodic review and that nothing can grow without proper nurturing, care, and attention.

Any company or organization is like a tree. It seemingly looks the same each day but sheds leaves, lets its limbs rot, and applies band-aid surgery to its branches late in life. Therefore, it does not fully grow and bloom. Often, it dies an early death.

Give the organization the proper nourishment, and it will experience a growth process that is planned, steady, optimally profitable, and a pleasure to watch bloom.

Neglect it, and the tree (organization) will wither and eventually die. As the tree declines, it becomes a blight on the environment, harming its components and the neighboring grounds and flowers.

Understand the business in which you are really engaged. Trees seemingly look the same, but they're all different. They do not have the same purposes at comparable times in their developments. The nature of core business changes with time and should be steered, rather than evolve on its own.

Delineate how and why your organization operates. Trees are composed differently, with parts and structures relative to the environment in which they attempt to grow.

Perform multi-systemic therapy often. Without the proper care, trees (companies) will wither. Without continued care, they will die. With proper care, they indeed will blossom. If leadership addresses problems in every realm as they come up, rather than selectively ignore some, the growth process will be unhampered. With continued care, trees inevitably sprout deep roots and live a richer life.

The costs of remediation malnourishment, deterioration, or damage are six times those of properly feeding the tree (organization) on the front end. Human beings being the way we are, few of us do everything perfectly on the front end. The art and skill with which we remediate difficulties—sooner rather than later—constitutes longevity in business.

Which branch am I on, one might ask. Most people working in large organizations do not fully understand each branch, the interrelationship of each branch to one or another, or their own role as relating to the overall tree. For years, I've believed that, if you shook the branches of the tree, people would fall out, land on the ground, and then would climb back onto other branches, meaning that they would assume different jobs in different company niches.

The tree analogy applies to any kind of living, breathing organization, whether it is a corporation, healthcare institution, school, small business, non-profit agency, retailer, professional services firm, community volunteer group, professional association, partnership, or collaborative joint ventue.

Following the insightful examinations offered in this book, the ideal company would hopefully pursue a thoughtful strategic planning process. As a result, each company could make the following answers to questions posed above, per categories on the Business Tree:

1. **The Business You're In:** You are in the best business and industry; you produce a quality product or service and always lead the pack. Your customers get from you what they cannot really get elsewhere.

2. **Running the Business:** The size of your company is necessary to do the job demanded. Operations are sound, professional, and productive. Your standards, integrity, and dependability assure customers and stakeholders that you will use your size and influence rightly. You employ state-of-the-art technology and are the leader of your industry.

3. **Financial:** Keeping the cash register ringing is not the only reason for being in business. You always give customers their money's worth. Your charges are fair and reasonable. Business is run economically and efficiently, with excellent fiduciary procedures, payables-receivables practices, and cash management.

4. **People:** Your company is people-friendly. Your people are the organization's most valuable commodity. Executives possess good leadership skills. Your staff is empowered, likeable, competent, and loyal to the overall tree (organization). Employees demonstrate initiative and use their best judgment, possessing and demonstrating the authority to make the decisions they should make. You provide a good place to work. You offer a promising career and future for people with ideas and talent. Your people do a good day's work for a day's pay.

5. **Business Development:** You always research and serve the marketplace. Customer service is efficient and excellent, by your standards and by the public's. You are sensitive to customers' needs, and are flexible and human in meeting them. Marketing is truthful and reflects the strategies that you have worked so diligently to nurture. You sell what you can deliver. Management decisions are made with the customers clearly in mind.

6. **Body of Knowledge:** There is a sound understanding of the relationship of each business function to the other. You maintain a well-earned reputation and are awake to company obligations. You contribute much to the economy. You provide leadership for progress, rather than following along. You develop and champion the tools necessary to changing with the times.

7. **The Big Picture:** You approach business as a *body of work,* a lifetime track record of accomplishments. You have and regularly update and benchmark strategies for the future, maintain a shared company vision, understand that ethics is good for business, and "walk the talk."

In many companies, these things do not occur because people do not know the processes to enable them to occur. In some, a rigid adherence to egos and the old ways precludes success. Often, the wrong people are giving advice and have the ear of top management. Management is out of touch and ego-driven to lead without proper help or advice.

Oftentimes, the company does not feel that it needs to change—that change is something that others need, but not them. Perceptions of current success overshadow the hint that winds will shift in the marketplace. Assumptions are false and overshadow reality. Thus, the company is not really in the right business anyway. Management is afraid to think "outside the box." The company culture is based simply upon being afraid and paralyzed to do anything new, creative, or proactive.

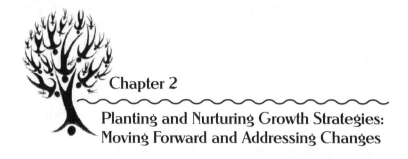

Chapter 2

Planting and Nurturing Growth Strategies: Moving Forward and Addressing Changes

Every organization and community in America is presently at a crossroads. Two current options exist. Business can be seen and known as a dynamic community that addresses its problems and moves forward in a heroic fashion—as a role model to the rest of the world. Or, the organization can bury its head in the sand and hope media attention dies down, thus becoming a generic tagline for troubled communities.

Preparing for growth is an ongoing process accomplished through a connected series of strategies and actions that will position any organization to weather the forces of change and thrive in new market environments. The process of evaluation, planning, tactical actions, and benchmarking takes striving for growth out of the esoteric and into routine practice.

This chapter expands the discussion toward assessing a business and creating strategic plans that can propel growth. The aim is to use the Business Tree model to craft strategies that are sufficient for managing expansion, locating new and expanded markets, identifying resources for expansion, evaluating the future of the industry, understanding competition and barriers to expansion, and preparing a rolling plan.

The rolling plan allows for revisions and adjustments. The creation of its components becomes a continuous exercise. The effect of changed circumstances, heightened demands, and supply conditions can be incorporated into the plan.

In fixed plans, annual reviews are made, but they are getting information regarding the progress of the economy. In rolling plans, the yearly reviews serve as the basis for the revised new plan every year. The uncertainty will evaporate because of the long-term investment decision of the company and its commitment of resources toward the plan.

First comes a rethinking of the overall business, its growth strategies, its purpose, its plans for the future, its mission, and its evolving corporate culture. This parallels the whole look of the Business Tree and how strategies will be nurtured through its branches, limbs, trunk, and roots.

Most trees (analogous to organizations) limp along because of their own unhealthy approach to life. They may not have been properly nurtured from the inception. Some were not meant to live long. Some were conceived for the wrong reasons. As a result, pruning and watering rarely ever occur. Preventive maintenance is seen either as a luxury or a threat to the status quo. They try to live and breathe just as other trees do.

Some trees are damaged by incidents not of their own making, but from which their health will be tested as to their ability to rebound. These include hurricanes, tornadoes, flooding, or drought (analogous to economic downturns). Normally recurring damages include heavy rainfall and snowfall. Other forces causing damage can include activity disruption on the lot (analogous to business forces outside their perimeters).

Some business trees are the result of overgrown root systems from other trees (spin-offs from other companies). There may be poison or disease in the soil (conditions such as lack of appropriate regulations and sanctions). Their livelihood could be threatened by the lack of deed restrictions or other neighborhood protection (failure to groom stakeholders and friends who could support the company).

Trees suffer neglect by professionals whom the owners contracted to nourish. They may be damaged because of treatments with the wrong equipment or supplies.

Harmful environmental factors include fads in site maintenance, which favor sparseness as a means of cost containment and a failure by the property owner to take ownership for any of these eventualities. This is analogous to consultants and staff members charged with upkeep of the company.

Planning on the front end is the answer to the question of organizational survival. Refusing to do so, companies instead apply surgery only when they have to. Damages are compounded when surgery is applied at the wrong time, too little too late, or applied to the wrong branches or by the wrong experts-consultants. Surgery that is nothing more than a band-aid does not relate to a thorough diagnosis or prescribed treatment.

To benefit from change and to grow, each organization must take actions to move forward. Understand where you've been and where you might go. Research the trends. Spot some opportunities. Predict and benefit from cycles in business.

Planting seeds in your Business Tree means heeding messages from the marketplace, revealing the changing conditions, new global business imperatives, and partnering concepts. With pruning and nurturing come the recognition of new stakeholders and other changes outside of the organization's influence that may profoundly affect them. Growth trees come from putting more focus upon running a successful organization.

Strategic Elements That Companies Do Not Address Until the Costs Pile Up		
Accountabilities.	Habits.	Processes.
Actions.	Learning curve.	Quality control.
Assumptions.	Operations.	Research.
Attitudes.	Opportunities.	Rumors.
Consequences.	Outcomes.	Skills.
Corrections.	People.	Strengths.
Egos.	Policies.	Successes.
Erroneous information.	Problems.	Threats.
Getting informed advice.	Procedures.	Weaknesses.

Stages in the Evolution of a Business

Just as trees and other environmental foliage grow at different stages in their existence, so do living, breathing organizations. As we use the number seven in this book as the parts of a whole, we also use seven as the sequential progressions that companies go through in moving toward successful growth, stability, and lasting presence.

These seven stages apply to small and mid-sized companies more vividly than to older established corporations. They are very experienced stages for examination of the whole of the organization and its functioning parts (departments, units, projects, and individuals).

1. **Transient Pleasure:** The company's founders are basking in the glow of initial achievements. An excitement exists over the founding mission and an understanding of current levels of expertise. The founders' creative instincts have been satisfied. Egos often get inflated because of the early bumps of momentum.

In the first year or two, the character of the organization has not changed yet. It reflects what it started out to be, with the first wave of people coming into the enterprise committed to a successful launch.

Unfortunately, the founders may have also brought along the excess baggage of the previous corporate cultures in which they worked. They don't want to be like company X, though, in swinging the pendulum in the opposite direction, they become more like the old company than they realize.

In the beginning, the founder projects his/her vision toward other people in the founding team. Pleasures are plentiful in the beginning because great responsibilities are to follow.

2. **The Big Letdown:** The machinery of the company must now perform on its own steam. The widget developer now becomes a widget producing and distribution organization. Some imperfections begin to reveal themselves, accompanied by some dissatisfactions and the inevitable blaming of others for mistakes.

The reality is that no fully compatible organization exists to handle growth at this point.

The founders cling to the notion of transient pleasure and wish to return to the early moments of success, or at least the perceptions of victories.

When management is willing to "stick it out," many strengths and an organizational character will soon be revealed. Founders must reaffirm their commitment toward themselves, their people, the organization, and the quest to make better widgets. They start seeing the company, its people, its processes, and its intellectual property as resources to be cultivated and not to be exploited.

3. **Times of Crisis:** ~~When mistakes begin occurring, the process of learning from failures must ensue.~~ Company principals recognize the end of the early illusions. Now, it's time to become more mature as an organization. Players must now determine if they are willing to make further sacrifices in order to go the distance.

   Just as we gain wisdom from the business failures and corporate scandals, we can learn equally valuable lessons from how the crises were successfully handled. The follow-through and crisis preparedness planning process help to divert other crises from transpiring.

   Every organization goes through various crises, and those that do not swiftly remediate the damages will sink into the pangs of a prolonged and painful existence. Research shows that 85 percent of the time, the scenario building for crises in the strategic plan will avert the crises from occurring.

   Purposes and expected benefits of reviewing business crises include understanding the difference between good and bad handling of crises and implementing methodologies to address problems sooner rather than later. By involving the widest base of support in proactive change and growth, the organization establishes safeguards against future trouble and puts more emphasis upon the positive ingredients and happenings in the community.

4. **Pain Follows Each Crisis Period:** In times of crisis, business does what it should have done earlier: study, reflect, plan, and manage change.

   Sadly, business often adopts a "head in the sand" mentality when the crisis seemingly passes. Many rationalize that they dodged the bullet. Some prefer to bask in and try to relive the early experiences, rather than focus upon the current crisis.

During the pain phase comes the band-aid surgery approaches that plague otherwise-clear thinking and planning. When it reacts to crises by overreacting, management begins taking the wrong courses of action. Certainly, trial and error is to be expected. Inevitably, band-aid surgeons usually pursue surface remedies for the pain, rather than addressing the root causes.

People who want quick, easy fixes only serve to prolonging the pain. Thus, they move from venture to venture. The realities of doing business for the long term have now set in. The failure of the quick fixes spurs management toward doing the things necessary to maintain staying power.

The character of the organization that seems to be emerging is now revealing itself. Things are not fun anymore, and some tough decisions must be made.

5. **Relief From Crises and Pain Result in Positive Periods, Known as Semi-Permanent Joy:** Unless management feels the pain and takes proactive steps to get through it, they will remain stuck in a rut. Those who think they are immune to pain and that they will remain in the pleasure mode are delusional and are doomed to long-term failure. The notion of pleasure and joy always being with the organization is a fatal flaw of corporate thinking.

    After enduring the crisis and realizing the extent of the pain, great managers start to study the reasons why they went through this process. They achieve the knowledge and understanding that an evolution has just transpired, of how things occurred, and of what this portends to moving forward. Effectively treating the pain and learning from it serves to reinforce the will and zest to achieve further.

6. **Assuring Future Success:** For long-term survival, it is important to give the seeds of creativity, planning, and organizational vision enough time, resources, and nurturing to sow.

Plan to grow the organization. Grow according to the plan. Craft a vision from the frustrations, mistakes, failures, missed opportunities, short sightedness, and self-sabotage that have crept in. At this insightful stage, the best leaders will learn from the failures of others in the marketplace.

7. **Understand the Truisms to Navigate Your Journey:** Having worked with thousands of CEOs (as clients, colleagues, and friends), I've absorbed many nuggets of gold. Some of these were taught to me as pieces of advice, experiences, and shared learning curves. Other pieces of wisdom were reality-based lessons from the marketplace. All steered successful business leaders toward courses of success.

Organizations do not set out to go bad. They just don't "set out" (little or no planning). Thus, they go off course.

There is a difference between knowing a product or industry and growing a successful business. Understanding all seven components of a successful company and the seven progressions of working through any problem is a concept that I call the Business Tree™.

Much of the wisdom to succeed lies within each organization. There is much knowledge in your employee ranks. It must be encouraged and utilized.

Much of the wisdom to succeed lies outside your company. Mentors must be called upon sooner rather than later.

People under-perform because they don't know what is expected and are not given sufficient direction, nurturing, and standards of accountability. Learning how to empower people, and give them recognition for good work and the encouragement to go the distance is a concept that I call the Organization Tree™.

Anybody can poke holes at an organization and criticize its activities. The art is to create programs and systems that recognize how much in the organization is really constructive. That is a concept that I call Three Rights Offset a Wrong.

It is important for management to communicate abstract principles in very concrete terms. The wheel of an organization must always move outward, establishing commonality and communicating with stakeholders, who are those affected directly or indirectly by your being in operation.

Whenever possible, try to counter balance left-brain precision for details with right-brain insights and creativity. There is a difference between knowing and feeling. The intellect (left brain) draws something to itself. The will-spirit (right brain) reaches out to something that it loves and aspires to do. Management should hear all shades of expertise and opinion in developing strategies.

People must continue to develop professionally in order for any business to grow. The more valuable a portfolio of knowledge they develop—much more than just skill sets—the more valuable is the company. Regardless of what they do in life, people learn things that can be applied. Normally recurring damages are effected by their career plateau. The Organization Tree signifies stages and progressions of growth in one's own career.

Raise the common denominator whenever possible. Whenever the mind knows something that is below, it elevates the knowledge.

When the will-spirit covets anything that is below itself, it is degraded. When people and organizations are obsessed with something beneath them (such as money and fame), the whole entity is pulled down.

When the will has aspirations and visions above it, standards will rise. It is important to have the right kind of heroes and goals because role-model status perpetuates throughout life and permeates organizations.

It is possible for a company and its managers to know much about certain arts and sciences without having the will to pursue them. The level of achievement by a company is commensurate to the level and quality of its vision, goals, and tactics. The higher its integrity and character, the higher its people must aspire.

One learns three times more from failures than from successes. The lessons must be reinforced, studied, and applied to future planning. That is a concept that I call The Fine Art of Failure.

Strategies in Creating Distinctive Value for Business Stakeholders

- ➡ You have more strengths than the others.
- ➡ Yours must be seen as a "demand" industry.
- ➡ Opportunities far outweigh the threats.
- ➡ Turn others' weaknesses into your threats.
- ➡ Nothing can grow without proper nurturing, care, and attention.
- ➡ Everyone has to market and promote the cause.
- ➡ Use experts from outside your industry.
- ➡ Champion change.
- ➡ Business and public stewardship are honorable public trusts.
- ➡ Being a role model, you become a better executive and leader.
- ➡ Success is more about building and sustaining relationships.
- ➡ Most of life's great secrets are found through creativity of people.

Organizations start to crumble when their people quit on each other. Giving up is not an option in a growth strategy. No organization can operate in a vacuum. Each needs bases of support, community goodwill, and collaborative business partners.

Unhealthy organizations will always "shoot the messenger" when changes and improvements are introduced. Healthy organizations absorb all the knowledge and insight they can, embracing change, quality improvement, and planned growth.

Developing Growth Strategies

A growth plan or strategic plan is a must for any organization that intends to survive and thrive in today's rapidly changing business environment. Look at the whole, then at the parts as they relate to the whole, and then at the whole again. Plan to grow, and grow by the plan.

Next is a profile of the core business, the ancillary business, and the outcomes possible by expanding business unit potential. It includes the management structure, operational facets, facilities, staff resources, time lines, organizational chart, and more.

If one believes the other books and consultants selling growth strategies, the key to growth lies within their specialty niche, whether it be human resources organization, training, technology, sales, marketing, coaching, or financial planning. This is simply not true. Instead, I contend that business owners and principals must analyze *all* aspects of the operation and use them *together* to promote a coherent vision for the organization.

For example, I have conducted numerous audits of companies that followed expensive branding programs sold by marketing consultants with the failure to deliver promised benefits. One involved a rollup of home service provider companies. They launched an expensive branding campaign to define their teams as appearing in a timely manner to get the gigs, selling immediacy as the benefit to calling them.

Focus groups showed that disgruntled customers felt that the rollups lacked the localized integrity of the predecessor companies. Yes, the new teams were on time to get the engagements but failed to do the follow-through in a timely manner. Thus, the marketing messages did not reflect the realities of company service.

I visited with commercial contractors in their quest to enter the home services market. We studied the pros and cons of small, localized, "mom and pop" contractors, as well as the services rendered by high-volume sales-oriented rollup companies.

The strategy emerged as a recommitment by commercial contractors that, in order to get the big contracts, they had to be "best in class." Because they were regulated and documentation-oriented, they would bring those same high standards to the work they did for homes and families as was expected of them in the commercial arena.

This recommitment to quality drove their work product, their customer service, and their business philosophies. As a result, their marketing messages, and the levels of customer satisfaction, retention, and referrals underscored their strategy. Many commercial contractors were then able to parlay their success rates in residential work as further assurance to corporate jobs of their attentiveness to service and quality.

One of the biggest growth areas is the rollup into extended service companies. Garden centers and home-improvement chains are nurturing preferred provider lists for landscapers, installers, and so forth. I am advocating more companies that aggressively seek the best providers and market their services as a holistic company with a high profile.

Another of the biggest growth industries, I predict, will be marketplace Websites that become online marketers of products, services, and processes not readily available to mass customer bases. With the success of eBay and Amazon.com, a host of niche-oriented Websites emerged. In most cases, a programmer started a company, picked a cause, and got experts in that niche to provide the resources for a successful Web-based company. Etsy, a Website that sells handmade clothing goods, does more than $100 million in annual sales.

I think there are still other marketplace-type Websites yet to be created. The ultimate clearinghouse for business professional services has yet to be created. In 1998, I came up with a concept, and it has yet to be initiated by some enterprising entrepreneur.

• ● •

Distinguishing your company from the pack always involves developing strategy first, with marketing as a subset that reflects the company's abilities to deliver the goods, put customers first, and reap referrals. Branding is a subset of marketing, which is driven and overseen by business strategy.

Planned, orderly growth for companies means generating constant, reliable ideas and creative approaches for management. It means understanding and adapting to external influences that profoundly affect the climate in which companies do business. A farmer's cooperative in the Midwest dairy industry noticed an erosion of their market share. Concerned over successful advertising campaigns by California and other states to carve market sectors for their dairy industry, this cooperative wrongly thought it was the job of government to get their business back. My observation was that such an impractical position would not serve to create a re-emerging business climate. Instead, the cooperative was advised to research other areas of the world where their products could find fame. They wisely decided to enter previously under-served markets, utilizing e-commerce. The resulting marketing of services by this proactive strategy was very successful.

Sadly, some executives and their companies eschew planned, orderly growth and choose to take other paths. In 1984, I was asked by a major corporate CEO to meet with and analyze the capabilities of a young, emerging business executive named Ken Lay. During the session, Mr. Lay asked me, "How can I buy instant credibility?" I replied, "You earn it the old-fashioned way. If one persists in taking shortcuts and cutting ethical corners, it will catch up with you. I strongly advise you not to go down that road and take it slow and steady." Mr. Lay said that he understood and respected my position, but did not take my advice.

With chagrin, I watched Enron's antics and predicted the company's downfall as far back as 1990, though its scandals and fall from grace did not surface until 2001. Thereafter, I wrote a dossier on the danger signs that Enron had displayed along the way. It included entering businesses beyond the core, taking unfair advantage of the supply chain, and incorrect community posturing.

After each round of corporate scandals, business and public officials always proclaimed, "There will be a time to go back and review what happened. That time is not now." I kept retorting, "If not now, when?" In my speeches and corporate retreats, I always reviewed the lessons that business should have learned from each wave of scandal and economic decline.

The fact that business persists in burying its head in the sand, denying the ethical lessons to be learned, and continuing to seek easy buttons is indeed why new waves of business crises keep occurring.

I have steered full-scope planning processes for hundreds of companies, and have conducted independent audits of previous plans and why they failed. Generally, I found them mired in trite phrases lifted out of pop culture or created as rationales for slanted, limited points of view.

By writing this book, I charge that enough of the old ways is enough. It is time to reflect and widen the focus upon where businesses live, how they operate, and where they are headed.

Imperatives for the New Order of Business

It is crucial for those who wish to survive to know and comprehend the business they are really in. Prioritize the actual reasons why you provide services, what customers you seek, and the external influences affecting your ability to do business. Where all three intersect constitutes the growth strategy.

Broaden the scope of your products and services by redefining the core business. Find new and creative ways to work with companies other than your own. Collaborations, partnering, and joint venturing enable the major business emphasis for economic survival and future growth.

Focus as much as you can upon customer service. Dispel the widely held expectations of poor customer service. Building relationships is paramount to adding, holding, and getting referrals for further business. Research shows that retaining 2 percent of customers from deflecting has a larger impact on your company's bottom line than cutting 10 percent out of operating expenses.

Plans do not work unless they consider input and practicalities from those who will carry them out. Know the people involved, and develop their leadership abilities. Plans must have commitment and ownership.

Markets will always seek new and more profitable customer bases. Planning must prepare for crises, profit from change, and benchmark the progress. "More of the same" is not a growth strategy. A company cannot solely focus inward. Understand forces outside your company that can drastically alter plans and adapt strategies accordingly.

Evaluate the things that your company really can accomplish. Overcome the "nothing works" cynicism via partnerships and long-range problem-solving. It requires more than traditional or short-term measures. He who upsets something should know how to rearrange it. Anyone can poke holes at organizations. The valuable ones know the processes of proactive change, implementation, and benchmarking the achievements.

Take a holistic approach toward individual and corporate development. Band-aid surgery only perpetuates problems.

Focus upon substance, rather than "flash and sizzle." Success is incrementally attained, and then the yardstick is pushed progressively higher.

Vision is an organization's way. Corporate culture is the methodology by which each organization can successfully accomplish its vision.

For companies to succeed long-term, the visioning process begins with forethought, continues with research, and culminates in a strategic plan, including mission, core values, goals, objectives (per each key results area), tactics to address and accomplish, time lines, and benchmarking criteria.

Corporate visioning goes beyond the strategic plan. It sculpts how the organization will progress, its character and spirit, the participation of its people, and the steps that will carry the organization to the next tiers of desired achievement, involvement, and quality. Companies spend six times more each year in performing band-aid surgery on ailing structures. The investment in planning and visioning will reduce the opportunity costs and preclude the need for so much unnecessary fixing of pieces of the problems.

The level of achievement by a company is commensurate to the level and quality of its vision, goals, and tactics. The higher the company's integrity and character, the higher its people must aspire.

Any company or organization must look forward in order to survive and succeed. The skill with which one analyzes plans and crafts its future makes the difference between the company merely surviving and moving forward in a growth mode.

Growth strategies are only successful when they come out of the development stage and into the weekly practice of business. There are no shortcuts.

• ● •

Components of a Business-Organization
(with their percentages per role-function-activity)

Branch 1. The Business You're In (10%)

→ Rendering the service, manufacturing the products (5%)

→ Core business abilities, specialties, skills, expertise (5%)

Branch 2. Running the Business (14%)

→ Administrative practices, procedures, operations, structure, review (4%)

→ Physical plant (3%)

→ Technologies (1%)

→ Equipment, supplies, systems (2%)

→ Distribution (4%)

Branch 3. Financial (10%)

⇒ Cash flow, forecasting, budgeting, trends (4%)
⇒ Equity and debt financing (1%)
⇒ Accounting and record-keeping (4%)
⇒ Banking and investing (1%)

Branch 4. People (28%)

⇒ Recruiting, hiring, and supervision (5%)
⇒ Human resources management (3%)
⇒ Empowerment, team-building (7%)
⇒ Training, incentives, involvement (10%)
⇒ Professional-executive development (3%)

Branch 5. Business Development (23%)

⇒ Corporate imaging (4%)
⇒ Perceptions and realities (1%)
⇒ Marketing (5%)
⇒ Sales (7%)
⇒ Promotional techniques, strategies (2%)
⇒ Tactical reviews, modifications (2%)
⇒ Marketplace sensitivities, adaptabilities (2%)

Category 6 (trunk): Body of Knowledge (8%)

Category 7 (roots): The Big Picture (7%)

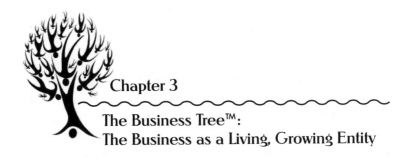

Chapter 3

The Business Tree™:
The Business as a Living, Growing Entity

Throughout many years as a business consultant, I kept getting called in to fix pieces of problems for companies. Most often, cutting expenses and having a new marketing program were the most common forms of band-aid surgery that they thought would solve temporary problems.

Companies thought that selling more of something was all they needed, rather than what they were selling, to whom, and the strains that increased volume and production capacity would have placed upon other sectors of the organization. I remember one where the marketing people and the salespeople would not communicate with each other, let alone coordinate activities. The results were increased sales with a multi-month time delay to produce products for a marketplace that was changing faster than was the equipment deliverability.

Through the years, I saw the wrong niche consultants being called in to fix the wrong problems, or what management incorrectly believed the problems to be. Most often, management was indeed the problem, or at least the logjam in the growth curve. The results were misspent funds, wasted efforts, and the subsequent scapegoat of the consultants for what the companies could not or would not do.

Years of observations and follow-up advisory work for companies taught me that the root causes of problems in companies must be addressed, rather than to continue performing rounds of band-aid surgeries. I also saw great nuggets of gold in those same companies, a bevy of talent, resources, and a willingness to make the changes, all of which could be positively brought to bear for the benefit of their business.

Rather than go in and criticize management for short-sightedness, bad policies, and wrong actions, it occurred to me that getting their companies back to basics and planning for the next strata would offer the opportunities to right the wrongs in the least judgmental matter. Proactive examinations followed by positively framed planning, to me, seemed to generate more results, foster more buy-in, and create new strategies than would the blame game.

Many times, I have been invited to present at board and management retreats. I always research the company, its products, its people, and its competition. By talking with industry opinion leaders, key customers, and other influencers, I always uncover gems that can be applied to new strategies.

The objective with companies is to reconnect present realities and opportunities with the visionary thinking that brought the company into existence. My "outside the box" material is presented as commensurate with enlightened thinking that had brought the company forward. I like to go out of the way to credit each organization's internal innovations. I have always recognized the emerging leaders of each company, thus requiring infusions of visionary strategy, practical applications, and the leadership quest necessary to climb the next plateaus.

The Business Tree™ is what evolved from doing many performance reviews, strategic plans, and management retreats. It is predicated upon change, growth, and adapting to outside influences.

This model takes as its premise that every organization is a growing, living organism rather than something resembling a pie chart, with every department and function seen as a neat, separate, digestible slice. It looks at business as a whole, then focuses upon each of the parts as they relate to the whole, and then back again on the whole. Look at the whole. Look at each part as it relates to the whole. Each part affects the behaviors of others and, thus, the whole.

The environment of a system affects the ability of its subset of parts to carry out successful functions. The parts of a system form a connected path, interacting directly and indirectly. The effect of any subset of parts depends upon the behavior of at least one other subset. A system is a whole that cannot be divided into independent parts without the loss of essential functions.

This model has been used as the basis for company performance reviews, business plans, reorganizations, and strategic plans that I have personally mentored. Through strategic planning, each part should see itself as it relates to the whole, not just to its own niche (as normally occurs in business).

With the tree symbolizing the organization as a whole, each major branch then represents a component of the company, such as finance or business development. Limbs on each branch constitute departments. Twigs are analogous to individuals who keep the organization running, both staff employees and outside consultants and other operators.

No single branch (or business component) can constitute a healthy tree (organization). None of the limbs (or components), twigs (outside suppliers and consultants), and leaves on each branch (employees) provide all the nourishment required to maintain the health and growth of the tree. Each branch has its proper responsibility and needs to interact with each of the others.

In visualizing the organization as a Business Tree, we began at the roots, Category 7, which represents the direction where the organization is headed, how it will plan to get there, and what factors, stakeholders, and opportunities will affect it.

Next, we focus upon the trunk, Category 6, representing the organization's body of knowledge, the relationship of the parts of the company tree to each other, and the factors outside the company that affect its ability to do business.

Categories 6 and 7 support, water, feed, and nourish branches 1 through 5. Naturally enough, the Business Tree will not stand without a trunk and roots. They keep the branches, limbs, twigs, and leaves growing. Trees with thicker bases and deeper roots will sprout greener (last longer, be more success-ful), shed less often (fewer corporate flaws), and live longer (dominate its industry).

Branches 1 through 5 are the primary components of the business and represent its five primary functions. The num-bers I've assigned them reflect the priority order in which most companies pay them attention, time, and resources. Branch 1 (core business) is not the priority number, but merely a start-ing point. Companies then mature their tree by nurturing the other branches in descending numerical order.

Branch 2 (running the business) takes a widget from Branch 1 and turns it into a widget production company. Branch 3 represents financial. Branch 4 embodies people, the most valuable and most overlooked asset of any company. Branch 5 stands for business development, which is directly intertwined with Branch 3, the fiduciary ability to stay in busi-ness. A direct relationship between sales, marketing, research, advertising, public relations, and customer service affects the financial strength of any organization.

Having conducted many performance reviews and com-pany valuations, I've learned that most organizations address only three branches at any given time, some effectively and oth-ers not so well. Usually, they make branches 1, 2, and 3—which should combine to 34 percent of the overall emphasis—into 100 percent of their focus, activities, and what they believed to be planning.

Traditional management consultants only know how to focus upon branches 1, 2, or 3. These include time-and-motion studies, just-in-time delivery, internal process controls, cost-cutting procedures, re-engineering, quality controls, and manufacturing. Traditional business models give short shrift to branches 4 and 5, the largest and most enduring branches in a growth company (51 percent combined). Further, they neglect to address the wider scope emphasis of categories 6 and 7 (15 percent combined).

These are reasons why businesses experience recurring problems, often requiring consultant services to fix. They wrongly think that a branding program is a panacea to fix employee problems. Branding is a sub-set of marketing, which is a sub-set of corporate strategy, not the other way around. I find myself contextualizing for corporate management the strengths that reside within the company, while debunking the wrong advice they have gotten from the wrong consultants. Excellent consultants need to sell their services in the wider picture perspective, in order to hold maximum value.

The organization that does not address all five branches and their relationship to each other cannot remain profitable. Further, attention must be paid to the trunk and roots, in order to remain standing in the long term.

Developing Strategies, Realizing Business Opportunities

Through the years, I have been brought in to help clients assess their business dreams and strategize their proclivities to come to fruition. Most of the realistic ones came true.

But what about the pipedreams that were more hype than substance? What did those who failed have in common? The emphasis was too much on having a copy of what someone else already had. The mousetrap they wanted to build was not fully delineated from others in the marketplace. Missteps coupled with such factors as under-capitalization, insufficient business partners, few stakeholders, poor timing, and inattentiveness to quality controls spelled missteps or disaster for those enterprises.

I met with the owner of a sandwich shop chain. He wanted to go public and establish a franchise organization. Turns out that putting a message on his napkins was the only way that he had to recruit franchisee inquiries. I very nicely held the "get real" meeting with him. I explained how a local restaurant chain goes national, citing case studies of the successful ones. I explained the process of going public, the funding that would be required, and the shifts in management style that would be necessary to transform an entrepreneurial mindset company and take it public. I detailed how other chains in his state and industry had tried and failed.

I asked for a statement of his core business values. The answers were whimsical reminiscences of growing up in another part of the country and transforming those foods to a national sensation. Never mind that several other sub shops had already cornered the market. His "draw the line in the sand" comment was that he would not make compromises on what he considered an ideal menu. I explained that turning local restaurants into chains and local chains into corporations involved everything but the cut of meat and that compromise decisions were the rule of business life.

I observed that his casual hometown hangout ambience was great for a college town, but too many changes would need to be made in the company in order to become a chain to rival other established players. My recommendations were to stay local, enjoy the local fun, continue maintaining his defined levels of quality controls locally, and be glad that he would not endure the headaches that would have been ahead in a publicly held company. He left the meeting feeling relieved. Who knows which roads those niche consultants would have taken his company down.

Business Tree lesson: Just because someone else has grown does not mean that all players in the same industry can expand rapidly. This company refined its core business to reflect a small company with standards that would have been changed in a rollout operation. They kept it back to basics.

• ● •

How many times over the years have communities stated boldly that they would become the next Hollywood, that they would establish Third Coast film production facilities, only failing to raise the necessary funds. I have observed many and even advised some major cities against trying for the distinction.

Business Tree lesson: No community can re-vision itself by adding one niche industry alone. The community that expends resources into being a copycat of other communities or hoping in vein that resources will come to support a dream will find itself coming up short.

• ● •

A group of doctor-owned ambulatory surgical centers needed to devise strategies to reach its full potential. Applying the Business Tree, we examined Branch 1 (core business), and we saw that the methods of healthcare delivery were changing and that such centers have proven to be a cost effective alternative to day surgeries at hospitals. Insurance companies and group health buyers were beginning to pick up on this and contract with ASCs as alternatives to more expensive hospitals for certain kinds of treatments. The insurers, rather than individual patients, were becoming the new customers that this client needed to target.

This set of circumstances resulted in changing Branch 2 (running the business). Doctor-owned hospitals were popular investments in the 1980s, but they gave way to the corporate-owned facilities. This ASC company was busy in packaging itself in order to sell to one of the for-profit chains. We researched other healthcare niches that the major companies did not own and decided that, rather than sell, this company would put together a rollup that included imaging centers, medical practice consulting arms, and other service providers. They purchased other healthcare companies to make the new entity more full-service and thus more attractive to the insurance companies. The plan of reconfiguring the core business and the way in which service companies would run worked.

Business Tree lesson: The formation of corporate strategies is itself a "work in progress." Often, going through the process of rethinking and planning encourages some companies to change directions, retool their core business, and broaden their business presences.

Communities as Living, Growing Business Enterprises

Entire communities can and must see themselves as business enterprises. When they make realistic, prudent efforts to diversify, grow, or come back, this involves a combination of strategies, resources, and people. Cities such as Las Vegas, Nevada; Branson, Missouri; and Orlando, Florida, did not attain their designated glories purely by accident. All put formerly small towns on the international map by taking planned community status and marketing toward much wider audiences.

Following the 1999 shootings at Columbine High School, the city of Littleton, Colorado, made a concerted effort to come back as a strong community. That meant mounting an economic development effort, fostering quality of life, and offering theirs as a beacon to communities set upon moving forward, putting themselves in a position to thrive at that next plateau.

When conducting leadership retreats for cities, I called attention to the overlapping and duplication of services by departments charged with planning functions. In each, there were three departments: one for real estate activities, one for roads and sewer infrastructure, and another for traffic. I suggested that the term *infrastructure* relates more to quality of life and services to citizens, beyond the scope of just sewers, roads, and bridges. Afterward, each city pursued a thoughtful process by staff that combined and expanded the planning functions to incorporate "quality of life" value to citizen services. The resulting cities achieved larger bond ratings, received positive marks for heightening citizen-friendly government, and were better poised to face economic challenges.

Northern industrial cities have had to diversify their economies in the post-industrial age. The city of Syracuse, New York, mounted efforts to attract research, healthcare, technology, and hospitality institutions into downtown hubs in order to re-energize its central city. I was invited to speak to citizen stakeholder audiences, giving case studies of how other cities came back from economic downturns, companies leaving town, loss of jobs, and the business demands to diversify. I was impressed by the commitment of business visionaries who expended the capital necessary to foster local growth strategies and community visioning. I was inspired by the sincere desires of local businesses taking steps to strengthen the local economy.

Similar formal strategies to take communities to the next plateau have formed all over the United States. The private sector and public sector can both learn from concerted planning efforts, generated by crisis but rooted in thoughtful planning. Although vertical cities have been losing population, mid-sized horizontal cities with high levels of educated workers have emerged as production centers in the technology age. These include Irvine, California; Austin, Texas; Chandler, Arizona; Boise, Idaho; Salt Lake City, Utah; and Raleigh-Durham, North Carolina. Austin, for example, mounted a concerted effort to create a technology corridor that subsequently drew more than 1,400 software production companies alone.

Other U.S. cities mounted visioning and planning efforts, thus attracting business, commerce, wealth, and prominence. These communities include Boulder, Colorado; Santa Clara, California; Park City, Utah; Jackson Hole, Wyoming; Silicon Valley, California; and Fort Collins, Colorado.

Large cities represent grounds for rebirths because they have large immigration populations, many of whom are knowledge workers. These include Houston, Los Angeles, Dallas, San Jose, Miami, Phoenix, Philadelphia, Atlanta, and San Diego. The economies of these regions display powerful opportunities to communicate, network, do business, and enjoy community life. The energy and work ethics of immigrants tend to inject further vitality into these communities. These formerly unattached new urbanities constitute the critical new blood for the post-industrial urban economy.

Every major city and country of the world should undertake strategic planning and visioning programs, in order to move forward. Globalization is the biggest challenge of our time, accelerated by the infrastructures of communication, where the transfer of everything from ideas and data to goods and services has now become a staple of everyday business. Globalization impacts the safety of our nations, value of our currencies, condition of stock markets, products we buy, customers we serve, and competition that we face.

The globalization process considers different cultures, practices, and dilemmas faced within the realm of international business. The challenge of business planning is to understand and relate to the rest of the world. Human creativity and resilience are our primary economic resources.

Global business is more about exporting products and services, rather than the exporting of jobs. Understand the world's cultures and that world history repeats itself. Study how the global economy works. Visualize the possibilities, including trade blocs, geopolitics, and strategic alliances. Interact with and help your customers develop their international activity.

I strongly recommend that every city and state governmental entity mount visioning programs, which incorporate strategic planning and much more. These are necessary for survival, usually create jobs, stimulate bond ratings, and result in partnerships that benefit each participant.

Hold Up the Mirror: Conducting Performance Reviews

My Business Tree model has been utilized in visioning processes. One state saw it as the basis to expand the scope of performance reviews. I do not use the term *audit* when conducting organizational reviews and company valuations. That term portends to financial and "time and motion" measurements only. Some consulting firms conduct audits because those are the limited measurements they know how to make. In contrast, I see a performance review as more than just trimming the fat and criticizing incorrect activities in the organizational structure.

The term *audit* brings to mind an anticipated doom and gloom once the results are released. I recommend that it be replaced with a performance review, this being the precursor to the next strategic planning process. Such a formal review is a wider-scope look at all factors that contribute to an organization's well-being. That means putting more emphasis upon factors that traditional audits do not. That also entails identifying factors that already contribute well to the organization, rather than simply looking for ways to cut, curtail, or penalize.

This review is the basis for most elements that will appear in a strategic plan, including the organization's strengths, weaknesses, opportunities, threats, actions, challenges, teamwork, change management, commitment, future trends, and external forces. Among the components and professional specialties that could be represented in a performance review, per each branch on the Business Tree, include:

Branch 1:   Core business, core industry.

Branch 2:   Environmental, safety, IT systems design and computer software, training for computers and technology, architecture, engineering, and legal.

Branch 3:   Accounting, banking, investments, financial planning, benefits programs, real estate, fund-raising for non-profit organizations, and investor relations services for public companies.

Branch 4:   Training for diversity, team building, professional education and development, and motivational and executive development-mentoring. Human resources administration, employee testing, behavioral research, executive search, talent pools, reorganizations, downsizing, executive outplacement, labor issues, and negotiating.

Branch 5:   Sales strategy, sales training, marketing strategy, customer service, advertising, direct marketing, public relations, special events, video production, promotional specialties, graphic design-production, and Website design-production.

Category 6: Business performance reviews, research, quality management programs, government relations, public policy, community relations, and re-engineering.

Category 7: Corporate strategy, visioning, strategic planning, futurism, thought leader program, and emerging business issues.

Sample Performance Review Outline

Following the criteria just stated, here is a model of performance reviews that was created for school districts. Previous audits looked at what was taught, how it was taught, and the educational dynamics.

This expanded tree-like approach was beyond that of a "time and motion" traditional management study. Other subtexts of this study module included multi-cultural diversity orientation, relationships within the district communities, the effects of district activities upon public opinion, organizational development, community relations, leadership development, and long-term strategy.

1. Operations of the district:
   - Instructional programs since conversion to site based management.
   - Teacher certification and professional development.
   - Physical plants.
   - Resources, equipment, vehicles, technologies.
   - Outsourced contracts for school operations.
   - Relations with students and parents.
   - Administrative operations.
   - Financial controls, accountabilities.
   - Sources of revenue: taxes; non-tax and private sector support.

2. Community perceptions of the district:
   Study what they used to be and what they actually are today.
   - Explore what public support of education can accomplish.
   - Review bond elections and why they pass or fail.
   - Address the critics and turn some into supporters.
   - Inventory and showcase positive qualities and programs, in order to cast a more accurate and favorable light upon the role of education in society.

3. Teacher training, morale, and support:
    - Examine the levels of morale and how the situations came to pass.
    - Explore turnover, tenure, and departmental structures.
    - Recommend and identify sources for training and topics for in-service material.
    - Study ways in which students, parents, and administration can share in the empowerment process.
    - Foster mechanisms to recognize teaching excellence, service by teachers, and professional development.

4. Public-private partnerships:
    - Study presently available resources and trends.
    - Analyze the success to date of school support programs.
    - Determine niches in partnerships that have yet to be filled.
    - Recommend ways for businesses and citizens to get involved with schools.
    - Involve new and surprising sources of support, including teachers and students.

5. The district's future:
    - Study resources the district needs in order to survive and prepare for the future.
    - Make recommendations toward launching a visioning program.

As a result of this expanded scope of performance review, several areas were addressed that might not have been covered under a "reading, writing, and arithmetic" audit. Areas that received public attention and subsequent attention included the condition and safety of school buses, the food service operations (many of which were subsequently outsourced), safety concerns around school zones, the building of new campuses in older inner-city locales, and public-private partnerships (which raised more grant money and stakeholder support).

Grounding Factors for the Tree

Being stable does not mean that an organization stands still. Upholding traditions does not necessarily mean that one vehemently resists change. Being a family-run company does not mean that outside stakeholders do not exist.

Lawyers go to school to study the law, not how to become a lawyer and run a legal practice. The same analogy holds true for accountants, engineers, doctors, and architects. All are taught professional skills but must absorb along the way the business talents necessary to run their practices.

Authority figures must be effective disciplinarians. They must also be recognizable role models in order to inspire commitment from their team members.

The best leaders are adept at the balancing acts of business priorities. Organizations are collections of individuals, team clusters, operating units, departments, management philosophies, and ideologies.

To gauge the company's future direction and avoid roadblocks to success, independent performance reviews must be conducted. The objective is to benefit from changes, rather than become the victim of them. By spotting trends and recognizing inner strengths of your existing company, you can compete and excel more effectively than without any strategy at all.

Challenges, Trends, Opportunities for Business

1. **The business you're in.** Fewer safety nets, less reliance upon the old ways. Results-driven business. Competition and changing marketplaces. Deregulations. Industry segments.

2. **Running the business.** Downsizing. Creating new efficiencies. Home based business. Rules, responsibilities and ethics. Productivity through uncertainty.

3. **Financial.** Fluctuating economies. Global economic development. Economies without borders. Incomes of companies vs. earnings. Outsourcing and privatization. Accountability, measurements and benchmarking.

4. **People.** Societal changes. Workforce diversity. Generational differences. Age discrimination. Backhanded discrimination, detriments to diversity. Perceptions of a homogenous workforce. Education of the workforce. Team building and team links. Professional education, development and training.

5. **Business development.** Methods of communications. Niche marketing. Cause related marketing. Customer relations. Providing value-added. E-business. The court of public opinion.

6. **Body of Knowledge.** Intellectual property issues. Fear, failure, and success ratios. External influencers. Regulators and government relations. New understanding of organizations. Collaborating, partnering, and joint-venturing. Front-burner business issues. Institutionalization of rapid change. Growth strategies programs. Crisis management and preparedness. Executive leadership. Mentoring heir apparents and future executives.

7. **The Big Picture.** Growing necessity for long-term strategy. Strategic repositioning. Changing corporate cultures. Strategies and stages in management implementation. Worldwide competition for new ideas. Strategic planning and corporate visioning.

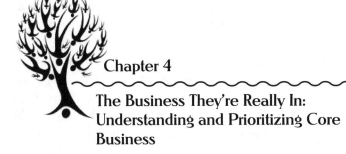

Chapter 4

The Business They're Really In: Understanding and Prioritizing Core Business

This chapter focuses upon prioritizing and realigning the primary reason for being in business. It is an in-depth look at Branch 1 of the Business Tree, the core of the business: how it is perceived, how it is developed, how it changes based upon marketplace demands, and what must be done so that company growth can continue. The rest of the tree cannot grow without this branch. It is who you are. It is what the business is to become.

All too often, companies fail because they are not crystal clear about what business their company truly is. Without that knowledge, the planning to sustain and grow is impossible.

Branch 1 is the easiest to climb onto. People get into businesses because they have expertise in one area, and if they are good at turning it into a business, they succeed. At the beginning of their work in the business, they are exceedingly comfortable with what they are doing.

Just as organizations start out to be one thing, as they grow, they often evolve into something quite different. What the founder started, if successful, will change through time and through generations of management. Disney started out as an animated movie studio, pure and simple. It has expanded far beyond that, and now its core business is licensing its name to retail outlets, cruise lines, credit card companies, ice shows, and more.

As businesses change, management must be astute enough to reshuffle its priorities. For example, the retail grocery store chain that has acquired so much property as it opened up stores—subletting space to other tenants—really must begin to run itself as a property management company. The local bistro that grew into a chain, found its core business becoming the selling of franchises.

I have worked with many businesses that had moved on from their original business model to something different as they grew and evolved. Case in point: the analytical instruments and equipment industry. Most of the niche companies in this area evolved and grew up because of chemical plant industrialization of the 1950s and 1960s. The founders worked in production environments where plants and factories had on-staff engineers, analyzer specialists, operators, lead chemists, and other technical department managers.

These professionals all came along in the same generation. They founded their companies to meet scientific niches. Their entrepreneurial efforts led to the research and development of the technology. They began serving a broad range of industrial, institutional, and governmental client organizations, providing specialized equipment and services to assure accurate analyses and process control.

Cutbacks at chemical plants, water treatment facilities, and such have all but eliminated the staff positions that utilize the equipment designed by these companies. Many of those people developed technologies at their plants and subsequently went into business to manufacture and distribute.

The client side changed, while many of these niche companies stayed basically the same. Throughout the years, factories, laboratories, and plants merged. Their numbers have shrunk. Cost efficiency became the overriding factor. In industry, the analytical equipment buying decisions are made by purchasing agents rather than technically trained supervisors. As a result, equipment is bought, and vendors are expected to install. There is not as much follow-through. Equipment and systems are less integrated than they used to be. The development of operating software is usually done in-house or with their own consultants.

Business Tree lesson: Rigidly adhering to the initial core business makes one impervious to the next generation of customer needs. No organization can remain unchanged and expect to succeed.

• ● •

To address the needs, many of these technology companies have moved beyond the making of equipment and into training customers in the use of the equipment, consulting on chemical issues, environmental audits, monitoring, and other professional services. I recommended that they expand their priorities toward selling consulting hours and contracting for projects, moving from being just a manufacturer to a consulting business. They were able to expand in such a way as to show customers the connectivity of all equipment to each other. The by-product of being inside the plants was uncovering other needs, which resulted in the development and modification of other equipment to serve necessary functions.

During my work with a chain of credit unions, which were attempting to move further into the banking business, several priorities had to be examined, in order to expand the notion of core business.

We asked some key questions: Would small customers still come first? How do we compete with established banking companies? What kinds of additional services must we provide? Where do we find customers in previously under-served markets?

Having advised various independent banks in developing their strategic plans, I saw some common themes emerging. Each of the independents had said it wanted to avoid falling into the pitfalls of the big bank holding companies, yet all of them wanted to grow very large. Achieving a healthy balance of strength, size of deposits, and customer focus with the credit unions was the strategy. The planning process fostered a culture that was commensurate with their rich history and the assurance of plenty customer service, enough to draw customers away from banks that had gotten too big.

Business Tree lesson: The organization that moves forward will serve new and expanded customer bases. Putting customers in the forefront of all management decisions and planning portends to the future of the business expansion.

Ranking by Priorities—Theirs and the Customers'

As companies evolve away from their core businesses as originally established by the founders, a profound dissonance can develop within the organization itself regarding what it is and what its priorities should be.

For example, as a company grows, top management will claim its number-one priority to be revenue volume and its rewards, including bonuses for key management. At the same time, actually delivering the core business as it is promoted to its customers slips to number 10 in the priority ranking. Increasing company revenue is priority number two, whereas customer service, or follow-up beyond the sale becomes number 12. No wonder that top management, company professionals, and workers find themselves pursuing differing goals, with inevitable conflicts that need to be resolved through planning, prioritizing, and realigning the core business.

This chapter identifies agendas and priorities in specific industries, showing that what they promote themselves as being to customers and the outside world is in reality very low on the priority scale within the organization.

Take energy companies, for example. Their number-one priority is marketing their products, whereas their number-two priority is profiting their investors and executives. Yet they promote themselves as being all about finding new sources of energy. Take school systems. The number one priority of management is to raise funds through taxes and grants. Yet they promote themselves as being there to help their students learn.

Frame of reference is everything in business. Different people within the same organization have contrasting views about the business they are really in (core business).

Organizations found themselves to become one thing, but they evolve into something else. In their mind, they're one thing. Other people think they are something else. The truth actually lies somewhere in between.

A company starts out to create the best widgets possible. After the art of building the first widget has been resolved, then the harsh reality of running a widget factory appears. People need to be trained to make and process widgets through the production chain. Other people must find and develop the widget marketplace.

Then come the onslaught of widget competitors and clones. The widget regulators get involved, as do the special interest groups.

Then, the widget company decides to go public. Selling stocks, raising capital, and working with the financial community become the priorities. Constituencies start complaining that the company has veered from its initial mission. It's no longer the mom-and-pop widget maker that it once was. It's become a corporation, or a bureaucracy, or a bunch of marketers, or a technocrat institution, whichever constituency the critic does not belong to.

The company is no longer in the business that the founder started. Each camp sees the business differently. The twain do not always meet within their own company. Turfs continue to be protected. Each niche believes its notion of core business is the one and only core business.

Therein lie the inevitable conflicts. Rather than try to inter-mingle differing contexts, organizations continue to mean different things to different employees. Sadly, however, most organizations do very little to resolve conflicts of context. Problems continue to fester, costing the organization several leaves, twigs, and limbs on each branch of its Business Tree.

This chapter on prioritizing and core business gives an average priority ranking for companies-organizations. In addition to generic organizational priorities, each business, market niche, and type of goods-services has industry-specific characteristics. These add further agendas and priorities to the general list. What they promote themselves as being externally is usually near the bottom of actual priority rankings, or perhaps a category unto itself. Included are some samples of organizational priorities in 30 key industries.

Ranking the Business They're In

Priorities change. Dedicated providers of the service stated in the original company mission become frustrated when they do not understand the reasons for the shifting priorities.

Often, what organizations say they are in external promotions to potential customers actually ranks low on the actual priority list. That occurs due to the agendas of individuals who guide the organization, departing from the core business for which founders were presumably educated and experienced. Add to that the harsh realities of doing business and staying competitive.

Here is an average priority ranking for the core business activity of companies:

1. Revenue volume and its rewards, including bonuses for key management.

2. Growth, defined as increasing revenues each year, rather than improving the quality of company operations.

3. Doing the things necessary to assure the revenue stream, including billings, sales, add-ons, and marketing. Keeping the cash register ringing, rather than focusing upon what is being sold, how it is made, and the kind of company it needs to be in order to sustain the growth.

4. Running an organizational bureaucracy.

5. Maintaining the status quo. Keeping things churning. Making adjustments, corrections, or improvements only occurs when crises warrant (band-aid surgery).

6. Amassing prestige, gratification, and recognition for the company and for certain leaders.

7. Furthering stated corporate agendas.

8. Furthering unwritten corporate agendas.

9. Courting favor with selected opinion leaders and stakeholders.

10. Actually delivering the core business. Making the widget itself. Doing what you started in business to do, what you tell the customers that you do.

11. Doing the things that a company should do to be a good company. Following the processes, policies, and procedures to make better widgets and foster a better organization.

12. Customer service, consideration for the marketplace, and follow-up service beyond the sale.

13. Looking after people employed by the company, in terms of providing training, empowerment, recognition, resources, and rewards.

14. Giving back to those who support the company, including customers, stakeholders, and communities in which the company operates.

15. Advancing conditions in which core business is delivered.

16. Walking the talk via ethics, values, quality, and vision.

17. Giving back to the industry and amassing a body of business knowledge.

People in the organization whose jobs fall under each priority have vastly different perceptions of the organization, its mission, their role, and the parts to be played by others. Some jockey for position to make their priority seem to advance higher. Some keep people on the lower numbered rungs in check, assuring that their priorities remain low. Some become frustrated because others' priorities are not theirs.

Other people build fiefdoms within the organization in order to solidify their ranking. Some do their job as well as possible, hoping that others will recognize and reward their contributions. Some do not believe they are noticed and simply occupy space within the organizational structure. Some try to take unfair advantage of the system. Others are clueless as to the existence of a system, pecking order, corporate agendas, company vision, or other business realities.

Until such time as a concerted effort to establish commonalties of purpose is made (known as a shared company vision), then organizational chaos likely will perpetuate. This negatively impacts productivity, morale, and the delivering of the product-service. Customers always suffer the side effects from companies in chaos.

Breakdowns per Type of Industry

In addition to generic organizational priorities, each business, market niche, and type of goods-services has industry-specific characteristics. These add further agendas-priorities to the general list. What they promote themselves as being externally is usually near the bottom of actual priority rankings or perhaps a category unto itself.

Based upon my years of research, advising these industries, creating strategic plans for the industries, and conducting performance reviews, here are some examples of organizational priorities, per key industry sector.

Retailers

1. Keeping the cash registers ringing.
2. Moving case lots of merchandise, to justify negotiated prices and bonuses.
3. Sales of products.
4. Marketing of the store.
5. Making it difficult for customers to return merchandise.
6. Providing customer service, as it relates to making sales.
7. Overall customer goodwill service.

In external promotions, they say they're:
GIVING CUSTOMERS ALL THEY WANT AND NEED.

Energy companies

1. Marketing products.
2. Profiting investors and executives.
3. Perpetuating a system, mindset, industry, ideology, bureaucracy.
4. Engineering.
5. Energy production.
6. Research and development.
7. Serving the marketplace.
8. Issues advocacy.

In external promotions, they say they're:

FINDING NEW SOURCES OF ENERGY.

Healthcare

1. Revenues, billings, fees.
2. Maintaining the industry's pecking order of respect, status, and deference.
3. Running bureaucracies.
4. Interface with insurance companies.
5. Patient care.
6. Professional association activities, publishing, and image enhancement.
7. Health and wellness public education.

In external promotions, they say they're:

OFFERING AFFORDABLE HEALTHCARE FOR ALL.

School systems

1. Raising funds through taxes and grants.
2. Perpetuating a bureaucracy.
3. Gaining acclaim and recognition. Priorities are directly commensurate to those of constituencies that the districts court.
4. Educating students.
5. Serving communities (taxpayer base).
6. Education for education's sake.

In external promotions, they say they're:

THERE TO HELP STUDENTS TO LEARN.

Media

1. Selling advertising.
2. Influence buying, selling, peddling, fostering myths-perceptions.

3. Entertaining audiences, in order to deliver numbers to advertisers.
4. Giving the appearance of serving the public, to create cause-related marketing revenue stream.
5. Informing and entertaining audiences.
6. Serving the public as a community or public service.

In external promotions, they say they're:
CARING AND COMMITTED TO SERVING COMMUNITIES.

Elected public officials

1. Power, prestige, influence.
2. Championing own pet causes-issues-agendas.
3. Serving pet issues of selected constituencies.
4. Fundraising and other details of winning elections.
5. Serving general issues of overall constituency.
6. Advocating for the rights of those in need.

In external promotions, they say they're:
CHAMPIONING THE CAUSE OF FREEDOM EVERYWHERE.

Municipal bureaucracies

1. Real estate trade, expansion, taxation.
2. Serving special interests, overtly or covertly.
3. Maintaining a bureaucratic structure.
4. Furthering the agendas of bureaucrat managers.
5. Serving taxpayer needs.
6. Providing a forum for taxpayer issues.

In external promotions, they say they're:
RUNNING EFFICIENT GOVERNMENT.

Insurance companies

1. Revenues from policy sales.
2. Policy renewals with minimum of marketing effort.
3. Paying for their organization to operate.
4. Paying a network of third-party administrators.
5. Denying as many claims as possible.
6. Serving clients.
7. Paying claims.

In external promotions, they say they're:

PROTECTING POLICYHOLDERS FOR ALL EVENTUALITIES.

Consultants

1. Generating billings.
2. Marketing to get work; making claims and promises. Telling clients they require what consultant sells, rather than overview of client needs-realities.
3. Hiring support personnel after the work is obtained.
4. Client service.
5. Professional development, in order to be all that was claimed in the marketing.
6. Running the consultancy as a business.

In external promotions, they say they're:

IMPROVING BUSINESSES, PER THEIR NICHE DEFINITION.

Airlines

1. Filling the maximum numbers of seats at highest negotiated rates.
2. Competing with travel agencies to get customers to book directly.

3. Influential forces in communities and government entities.

4. Well-maintained fleets of equipment.

5. Well-trained and well-managed employees.

6. Committed to continuing customer service.

In external promotions, they say they're:

THE BEST TRANSPORTATION BARGAIN AROUND.

Entertainment industry

1. Selling tickets to events, copies of product, and repeat business.

2. Image marketing, to attract customers, glamour, and attention.

3. Revenue enhancement from sales.

4. Running companies to produce, package, and market products.

5. Show business...often smoke, mirrors, egos, and sizzle.

6. The entertainment product itself.

7. Customer enjoyment, catering to customer wants, fancies, and trends.

8. Corporate sponsorships.

9. People who produce, distribute, and market the products.

In external promotions, they say they're:

ASSURING THAT A GOOD TIME IS HAD BY ALL.

Computer and software companies

1. Vendors of products and consulting time.

2. Developers of sellable products.

3. Teachers of how to use their products.

4. Offer backup support to continuing customers.

In external promotions, they say they're:

PROVIDING FULL-SCOPE BUSINESS SOLUTIONS.

Telecommunications

1. Selling equipment.
2. Selling additional features.
3. Marketing company image, to help sell additional features.
4. Billing customers for add-ons.
5. Government relations; lobbying with opinion leaders.
6. Company agendas and administration.
7. Technology production-distribution-maintenance.
8. Customer service, as it relates to selling more products and features.
9. Customer service, as it relates to taking care of what was sold.

In external promotions, they say they're:

A PUBLIC TRUST; A HUMAN MOTIVATOR.

Restaurant (one location)

1. Creating and serving food recipes they have perfected.
2. Making a fair profit, though driving force is food quality.
3. Taking personal care of customers.
4. Overseeing details to maintain restaurant consistency.
5. Marketing the restaurant.
6. Administration of the business.

In external promotions, they say they're:

A UNIQUE DINING EXPERIENCE.

Restaurant chain

1. Opening new locations.
2. Realizing profits on all units.
3. Attracting investors for the next deals.
4. Edging out the competition.
5. Policies of uniformity and consistency.
6. Marketing of products, locations, and chain image.
7. Ambience and atmosphere.
8. The food product itself.
9. Customer service.
10. Vendor-supplier activities.
11. Staff training; employee relations.

In external promotions, they say they're:

A DINING EXPERIENCE THAT IS STANDARDIZED.

Public lotteries

1. Raising funds to pay for their own salaries, overhead, and bureaucracy.
2. Selling false hope to people wanting to get rich quick.
3. Preying upon people who want instant riches.
4. Selling an addiction (buying tickets) to those who can least afford it.
5. Administering the process.

In external promotions, they say they're:

RAISING FUNDS TO BENEFIT EDUCATION AND OTHER POLITICALLY CORRECT CAUSES.

When They Say:	They're Usually:
Proven innovative concepts	Process upholders—nothing new or outside the box
Mission statement	Setting their own barriers—not full-scope planning
Growth opportunities	Sales goals-quotas (Market share is all that matters.)
Solutions for business problems	Suggestive selling for their products
Partnerships	Computer links to sales contacts
Information for customers	Sales promotions on their products
The next generation	Planned obsolescence of current-future models
Business services	Vendors of products
Planning-management consultants	Software peddlers
Fastest growing	Oriented to sales, not service or follow-up
Serving all your business needs	Peddling one concept (their product-service)
Fast, easy results	Selling quick fixes, not long-term solutions
Insightful advice	Suggestive selling for their products
Making life easy for the customer	Quick fixes, not in tune with your true situation
A perfect organization	Not acclimated to continuous quality improvement

The Business They Could Be In

Within any industry and company, wide priorities exist. Board members and line workers have different rank orders. Therein lies the rub—and the inevitable source of conflict within every organization.

Rather than wish for what we think "used to be" or "ought to be," the challenge is to reconcile differences of opinion and create a unified organization. Because priority rankings will rarely be identical among employees, the purpose of shared company vision is to build commonalties.

Here is a great case study, one of the proudest of which I was associated with. Cities along the U.S.–Mexican border were experiencing unemployment rates up to 28 percent. It was evident that the old hospitality economy model was obsolete. Downturns in ranching, farming, and energy led to the need to rethink the region's core business. The result was the Maquiladora industrial development program. Maquiladora means "made by hand" in Spanish.

This program was rolled out to a community in search of jobs and the positive feelings of better times ahead. It carried the theme "You Can Believe/Puede Creer."

It set up enterprise zones and attracted companies that performed light assembly work, especially in emerging technologies. This industrialization program built Laredo, Texas, into a manufacturing community, setting up hundreds of supply-chain relationships. This project resulted in major factories being built in Laredo, Texas, and Nuevo Laredo, Mexico, occupied by General Motors, Ford, Sony, Hitachi, JVC, 3-M, Stokeley Foods, and others. This lowered the unemployment rate from 28 percent to 13 percent.

The success involved community factions coming together to pursue a common goal. They courageously redefined the community's core business priorities. The cities became a genuine team, thus demonstrating that collaborations can produce larger slices of bigger pies for those who participate.

Business Tree lesson: The core business (Branch 1) of any municipality must see itself as economic and people investments, not just as a traditional infrastructure of streets, roads, sewer lines, real estate, stores, and buildings.

• ● •

As commerce becomes more dependent upon non-material products, the characteristics of intellectualism and independence, and the ability to construct economic relationships make the cities of the future more attractive. Where urban culture meets the frontiers of commerce, then the opportunities will build the communities.

Increasingly, cities are pursuing aggressive economic development programs. They are trying to attract enterprises. Our society is undergoing the social restructuring of labor markets. This is marked by the growth of high-skilled occupations, the growth of semi-skilled occupations, precarious and flexible employment conditions, and growing job migration. The new class of service providers requires career-oriented, well-educated people who are obliged to perform well and to keep growing as professionals.

The metropolis of the future will be a geographical intersection for production, finance, and control in an increasingly trans-national economic organization. This metropolis must adopt the world city hypothesis.

Core values of thriving organizations of all sizes should portray themselves as a place or turf, as shared ideals and expectations, as a network of social allegiances and stakeholder ties, as a collective framework, reflecting diversity and pursuing the common good.

Chapter 5

Preparing the Business Tree for Growth: Branches and Progressions Toward a Successful Company

Once management is certain that it knows what business it really is in, whether it is something similar to or different from the founding idea, the next step is to determine the best ways to run all parts of the company.

Returning to our tree metaphor, once we understand Branch 1 (which represents 12 percent of the total company), the core of the business, we must turn our attention to the rest of the branches, which are constantly changing and growing, and in need of our continual help in order to grow strong and stay healthy. Only then will a widget *maker* turn into a widget *business,* which may eventually become a widget *corporation.* The next possibility becomes a widget company rollup.

When experts start any company, their expertise usually begins and ends with the specialty and technology of their product. They generally do not know the most effective and efficient methods for manufacturing the device or delivering it to the marketplace. Nor will they understand the multiple dynamics of actually operating an organization. They have not been schooled on creating and sustaining corporate cultures, getting the most of the workforce, taking the company to new tiers, and standards of benchmarking the progress.

Far too many decisions affecting the growth of companies are made from the Branch 1 (core business) perspective. As a client told me, "We have to stop thinking like engineers. We're running a company now." And he was exactly right. When they do start thinking differently, they begin to see the business in a totally different light. Their planning and strategies must embrace an understanding of the parts or branches, how they relate to each other, and how they all work together to create a living, growing business—or, in a metaphor, a healthy tree.

This chapter is devoted to explaining the resources necessary for sustaining each branch of the tree, as well as describing the number-one illness that threatens the health of each branch, as I've encountered them in the many years of tending to such businesses.

Branch 2: Running the Business

This is the production, distribution, operations, and administrative side of the business. Branch 2 represents 12 percent of the total company.

Production includes the design, implementation, operation and control of people, materials, equipment, money, and information necessary to achieve objectives. Operations management refers to the goods produced or service-producing activity of the organization.

The traditional models stem from the age of manufacturing management. In the allocation model, resources are budgeted toward objectives. Network models follow the planning and controlling of projects. Inventory models ask how much will the company produce and when it is needed by customers.

Looking holistically at Branch 2, the systems approach factors the demand for goods and services into the planning, organizing, and control functions. Inputs include human capital, money, and raw materials. The work is performed through facilities, technology, and processes. The outputs are goods and services. Many random events affect the productive transformation.

The biggest problem facing this branch is that its organization may not be properly prepared, trained, or equipped to handle the rapid influxes of business. If production and deliverability are strained already, the situation will get worse.

In order to run it properly, this branch requires a highly trained staff, associates, and sub-contractors, including non-core business suppliers, equipment vendors, computer hardware and software companies, communications and technology providers, real estate-property-project management, retailers, wholesalers, purchasing services, and repair-maintenance companies. Primary consultants who may aid in keeping the branch healthy include lawyers, engineers (industrial, mechanical, process), and technology and systems analysts.

Business Tree lesson: Creative people say that running the business diminishes the spark of the early enthusiasm. I say that it makes a sensible widget company, with policies, procedures, and processes to assure staying power. No company can do all that it is capable of doing without infrastructure and sage controls. There is an art to good operational management, which serves as impetus to the rest of the tree's growth.

Branch 3: Financial

No company stays in business without money incoming and, one hopes a lesser degree, money outgoing. Branch 3 represents 10 percent of the total company.

Financial management represents the effective acquisition and use of money. This process includes estimating cash outflows and cash inflows. Comparisons are made to determine how to invest excess cash and ways to reduce outflows and/or increase cash inflows. The company identifies and compares outside funding sources, while establishing systems to monitor and evaluate the flow of funds.

The number-one illness affecting this branch for many companies is that it grows to too much prominence and begins to dominate the tree. Making money—increased revenues, new sales, and heightened profits—should not become the only driving forces of the company. Focus should remain on being very successful at providing your product or your service, protecting the business you already have.

Financial experts populating this branch allow the Branch 1 founders to stay focused on their fiduciary responsibilities. Staff, associates, and sub-contractors include MIS consultants, data processing companies, insurance companies, collection agencies, brokerage firms, business brokers, and financial support companies. Primary consultants working in Branch 3 include accountants, bankers, venture capitalists, and investment advisors.

Business Tree lesson: Companies that fear the budget and look only toward financial scorecards will lose sight of the rest of the tree. There are about 20 reasons for staying successfully in business. Earning sufficient profits is one of them.

Branch 4: People

This is the largest (28 percent of the total company), most important, and most under-nourished branch on the Business Tree. People can make or break a company. Disgruntled employees leaving with inside secrets can take that intelligence elsewhere. The care and nurturing of employees into constant, stable contributors to company success should be the major emphasis of every company.

Organizations cannot operate without people, yet employees often tend to be misused. There are so many problems associated with the handling of people in an organization that it is impossible to identify only one major illness threatening this branch. Too many staffs have been taught that corporate growth is the most important objective—eclipsing quality, integrity, service, and long-term sustainability—and are not empowered to make decisions or to take risks.

Employees who look only at their niche jobs and their tasks at hand do not see themselves as part of the overall company strategy. Far too many people in the organization are hired for their Branch 1 core business expertise but then are put into an administrative or operations role in the company's Branch 2 infrastructure. For example, engineers in energy companies often do not understand that the core business is energy marketing, rather than exploration and production. If kept in a myopic focus, they produce products and market without the skills or enthusiasm necessary to lead their companies.

All too often, when a company runs into trouble, management blames the employees when they themselves are a large part of the problem. Research conducted by the Harvard Business School shows that 92 percent of all company problems stem from poor management decisions.

Employees need lots of professional attention, grooming, mentoring, training, and administrative support. Research shows that the current workforce needs three times the amount of training than they are currently getting in order to remain competitive and productive. Too many companies give technical training but do not offer instruction on critical thinking skills, people empowerment skills, customer focus, leadership reasoning abilities, and the insights needed to project each person's job toward the greater company goals.

There are presently five generations in the workforce: "greatest" (those born prior to 1928), "silent" (those born between 1928 and 1945), "boomers" (those born between 1946 and 1964), "generation X" (those born between 1965 and 1983), and "millennial" (those born after 1984). Each generational grouping has its own characteristics, sets of working styles, life experiences, professionalism, and attentiveness toward quality. Few ever get their needs satisfied, resulting in reduced work output, a less-than-zealous attitude, decreased loyalty to the company, and a lack of interest in buying into management's ideas and goals.

Most managers need to refine their people skills and evolve into leaders. They must embrace empowerment, team-building, and open communication, among other concepts, in order to relate better to human beings.

Staff, associates, and sub-contractors in Branch 4 include trainers, employment agencies, staff leasing companies, out-placement firms, healthcare providers, workshop facilitators, seminar presenters, and executive services. Primary consultants supporting these people and resources include organizational development consultants, training companies, human resources consultants, mentors, and business advisers.

When companies extend the best resources to their staff, they are heralded as unique. One of the best (SAS Software) sustains a campus that has self-contained amenities. People are given the resources necessary to work longer hours, realize their full potential, and contribute to higher levels each year.

I became aware of the need for a stimulating environment through work with healthcare clients. One pioneered employee assistance programs, recognizing the fact that each troubled employee has a negative impact on 20 others. The goal to remediate problems in employees was met by offering substance abuse treatment. The vision was a more productive employee group.

I then saw the trend toward corporate fitness programs realize direct benefit to participating workers. Institutes of preventive medicine, storefront healthcare clinics, and specialist referral networks are businesses that have grown in recent years to meet needs not previously served by companies or traditional healthcare systems.

A large client of mine was concerned about absenteeism by employees related to their young children. One of the first corporate daycare centers came about as a way of keeping the parents on campus, offering visitation opportunities and a linkage to healthcare services. We researched daycare providers with whom to team. My recommendation was to partner with a large, local, non-profit organization, rather than with a commercial daycare chain. My hope was that the precedent of giving grants to community programs would enable those public sector agencies to grow, which it did.

By offering the best of the local community programs to the employee families, we saw increased confidence, reduced absenteeism, and a pride that the company really cared about its people. Because we linked to the non-profit world, this had enormous community marketing value for the sponsoring entity. The company did right by the employees and their children, and it was good for business. It inspired other corporations to follow suit.

Given that experience, the next step was to work with non-profit organizations to help them realize the opportunities to expand their services into corporate communities. The non-profit culture is seemingly at odds with the corporate culture. Non-profit people are oriented toward simply rendering social services and frame everything in terms of benefits to humanity. They hate to sell and regard fundraising with disdain. Most do not see themselves as business-like entities, which they really are.

The strategy was to engage board members from the business world to become advocates. After all, the thriving non-profit organization should be a hybrid of qualities, including fiduciary accountability, oriented toward meeting emerging needs and sharing much in common with local constituencies. The program showed how much the corporate community needed the best daycare and that partnerships to provide it were an honorable trust. Recruiting more forward-thinking board members and retraining staff on best business practices ensued. The results were expanded programs to corporate communities, with participating organizations realizing they had more in common than previous misconceptions had allowed.

Business Tree lesson: Nurturing corporate cultures always benefits every element of the tree. A productive Branch 4 (people) constitutes a more loyal, attentive, and productive workforce.

Branch 5: Business Development

Promoting and communicating about the organization are the main activities of this branch (which represents 23 percent of the total company). Companies stay in business by marketing and selling something.

Branch 1 core business creators think incorrectly that they are in the widget business. Actually, they are probably in the widget manufacturing and marketing business but fail to recognize and understand the business development part. Having a better widget is but a small part of the equation. Unfortunately, Branch 1 experts tend to undervalue marketing and sales, looking upon those professional specialties as necessary evils and not wanting particularly to deal with them.

Astute upper management will realize that giving life to a product or service is not the end of the job but rather the beginning, and will make sure that the importance of Branch 5 to the continued growth of the Business Tree is recognized and nurtured throughout the organization.

Why Employees Don't Perform

1. They don't know why they should do it.
2. They don't know where to begin and end.
3. They don't know what they are supposed to do.
4. They don't know how to do it.
5. They think they are doing what is necessary.
6. They think their way is better than what the boss or the rules suggest.
7. Something else is more important to them.
8. They are not rewarded for doing—just punished for not doing.
9. They are rewarded for not doing anything—and punished for innovating.
10. They think they cannot do the tasks at hand or are not up to bigger challenges.

Why We Don't Get Profitable Action

1. The organization does not plan for change or success.
2. People do not identify with objectives of the organization. They just work for a paycheck.
3. People are not empowered to feel important as contributors toward desired results.
4. People are not sure where they fit into the overall structure and mission.
5. Follow-up systems are not implemented.
6. People do not clearly understand what they are expected to do.
7. Goals are either too large or non-communicated.
8. Managers do not set enough of an example.

How to Get Profitable Action
1. Know the organization's mission, goals, tactics, and methods to achieve results.
2. Know job responsibilities, performance standards, and contributions toward the total effort.
3. Procedures, regulations, scope of work, and ramifications are communicated to all.
4. All employees have accountability for their actions, including mistakes.
5. Fair, consistent supervision encourages and recognizes correct actions.
6. Training is provided. Training develops critical thinking and leadership skills.
7. Latitude is given to exercise judgment, supported by management.
8. Everyone is encouraged to express ideas and suggestions, followed by consensus.
9. People mentor others, learning from professional experiences.
10. Empowerment enables the organization to accomplish something worthwhile.

I worked with a large homebuilder who needed a new message. The four factors of marketing are product, place, price, and promotion. My recommendation was to redefine the product and where it would be sold. We studied communities served by competitors and found the usual suburbs as the focus of business. Following research, we recommended that they go to places other than where their competitors were. The result was an expansion into minority markets for affordable new housing and smaller cities that were not being served by large homebuilders. The price and promotion grew out of the strategies of what and where to build, with the theme "The Future Has a New Address."

Trade and professional associations represent the cream of the crop in their respective industries. While helping members with professional development, regulatory issues, and business support services, all associations must conduct public education about their industry. The good guys must always distance themselves from the violators, demonstrating levels of integrity that are nurtured by association involvement. The National Roofing Contractors Association got a commitment from its state affiliates to work together in support of public projects. The result was a strategy of organized contractors working more closely together, signified by a cause related marketing project with the theme "All Over America."

Business Tree lesson: Had these processes been generated first by marketing, rather than big-picture strategy, they would have fared much differently. Cohesive business strategy must always be the umbrella under which promotions and business development fall.

Under Branch 5 (business development), staff, associates, and sub-contractors include sales managers, sales implementers, sales trainers, market researchers, marketing managers, marketing implementers, creative talent, graphic artists, graphics providers, audio-visual production, Web designers, printers, special events planners, specialty advertising companies, and direct marketing, telemarketing, and entertainment-incentive-promotional companies. Consultants include corporate communications consultants, public relations firms, sales and marketing consultants, business-to-business companies, and advertising agencies.

Branches 6 and 7 provide the inspiration, wisdom, nurturing, and strength that inspire the rest of the Business Tree's organizational branches to grow together as successfully as possible.

Category 6: Body of Knowledge

The tree trunk represents the organization's entire body of knowledge about the business itself and about all the outside forces that can affect the business. In a well-run company, it includes a set of processes for gaining new insights about the future of business, developing capabilities for growth and change, recognizing and analyzing emerging issues, and pursuing the next important steps.

The biggest problem here is that management usually does not take the time to understand how the company has grown or analyze the relationship of each branch, twig, and leaf to the others. They might put an accountant or a marketing person over long-term strategy, and that will result in a partial strategy based upon their branch orientation. Under those scenarios, successful change and growth become all but impossible. And it is unfair to blame a niche staff person or advisor for a partial overview.

The best planning is conducted by a visioning committee that represents all five of the major branches. It must cross-pollinate and factor strategies to the whole, not just to individual business unit niches.

As one of the few Category 6–7 experts, I spend much time counseling planners how to think bigger and develop techniques to open the focus beyond their branch orientations. This sophisticated and vital category includes research and consultation with management on external forces affecting company growth—mostly factors that are outside their control, but that can seriously affect and limit business opportunities. These include direct competitors, indirect competitors, regulators, governmental entities, horizontal marketplaces, vertical marketplaces, global business communities, and threatening socio-economic situations.

Business Tree lesson: This is all about knowing who your company's stakeholders are and how to mine them optimally. Companies that weather forces outside their company will fare better than those who underestimate forces at play.

Branch 7: The Big Picture and the Roots of the Tree

The really successful growth companies are the ones that take the time and appropriate the resources to develop a growth strategy. Down at the roots of the tree, business is approached as a Body of Work, a lifetime track record of accomplishments.

The healthcare system is focused upon treating sicknesses, diseases, and conditions. Many healthcare professionals advocate wellness, preventive, and public awareness programs. It is tough to get insurance companies to cover wellness programs. The system just reacts to and supports after-the-fact treatments.

My job with each organization is to widen the frame of reference as much as possible. Under a healthcare model, the corporate strategy symbolizes the internist, a diagnostician who knows about the parts and makes informed judgments about the whole. This enables the specialists to then be more successful in their treatments, knowing that they stem from an accurate diagnosis and prescription.

In business, I explain to senior management the concepts behind activities that employees and consultants are conducting. For diversity, team-building, sales, quality, customer service, training, technology, marketing, and all the rest to be optimally successful, they must fit within a context, a plan, and a corporate culture. Consultants have trouble in selling their worth to top management, and I often explain how their valuable professional activities fit into change and growth. There must be deep roots, in order to nurture a long-standing company. Everything leads to the roots and springs from them.

B usiness Tree lesson: Planning and full-scope strategy are the only roots that constitute meaningful growth. To assume that one can get by without a big picture is fool-hearty at best. Most often, it breeds failure into a paradigm that spirals companies downward. The best strategies reflect and involve each branch as an integrated strategy.

Intertwining the Branches

Companies go askew by taking predictable, usually wrong, courses. They may be attributed to actions taken on the wrong branch of the Business Tree, at the wrong times, and in the wrong order.

Each time a stimulus bailout hits the news, the discussion focuses only on infusing capital (Branch 3) and making cuts to expenses.

Discussion shifts to making corporate culture changes (Categories 6 and 7), yet it never seems to hit home. The system is so focused on budgets and fiduciary accountability (Branch 3) that it cannot refocus toward the other branches, where work needs to be done and changes made.

Each time a large retail chain closes stores and cuts outlets, it always cites poor locations as the public reason. The reality is that most expansion plans of retail chains are predicated upon availability of economical lease situations. Never mind that they did no market research (Branch 5) or analyzed competitors (Category 6). Never mind that they did not sufficiently test their product lines to see if they were still relevant to the marketplace (Branches 1 and 5).

The deciding factor for expansion is usually the availability of real estate (Branch 2). With all due respect to commercial leasing agents, they are not qualified to dispense business expansion advice. Nor should the real estate industry be blamed by large chains that did not do enough homework and research in order to enter or expand into new locations.

There was a community with three non-profit advocate groups devoted to encouraging citizens to become organ donors. Meeting with the newest one, I opined that three was too many and that one strong group could suffice. Non-profit groups often duplicate services, don't really work with each other, and compete for the same grants to fund operational resources.

This group was steadfast about staying in operation, rather than merging with others. They asked for advice in clarifying the core business. I asked, "Who takes the corneas to market?" The ensuing discussion evolved into an organ provider network that interfaced with healthcare providers.

Business Tree lesson: Changing the core business (Branch 1) inevitably changes the production and delivery of services (Branch 2). Refocusing their core business from the good intentions of citizen donors to the activities of healthcare professionals (reconfigured Branch 4) assured that the maximum number of donated organs would find recipients and that more would be served by this organization (expanded marketplace, Branches 5 and 6).

● ● ●

All of us who travel from city to city wonder where the locals eat. We wish that airport food would reflect the local culinary culture. The food court concept that had been popularized by shopping malls in the 1960s and 1970s finally came to airports in the 1980s.

I worked with a large city airport system. Up to that point, large food-service companies held the contracts, and the food was commonplace, was predictable, and offered little variety. With government bureaucracies being far too accustomed to awarding sole-source contracts, that practice precluded a food-court format populated by subcontractors.

We identified a company that would serve as a managing agent. Though they operated restaurants, their charge was to build and oversee a strong network of subcontractors. Thus, a realignment of companies (Branch 4) served to redefine the core business (Branch 1).

The mix of the products was based upon an objective panel of restaurateurs, hospitality industry veterans, hotel school faculty, and other experts concerned with building teams that would supplant a sole-source contractor. The committee sought out companies that would bring new tastes and diverse restaurant concepts to the food court. We realized that participation in this high-profile enterprise would put many small businesses on the map.

The committee judged menu items, plans for restaurant operations, and other aspects, followed by site visits to existing facilities. The recommended slate was presented to the city council for a vote. We proudly stated that 55 percent of the subcontractors were women- and minority-owned businesses. After achieving a winning vote, this coalition started serving at airport terminals, to great success.

Business Tree lesson: Collaborations, partnering, and joint venturing are the dominant trends in business today. The old model of a major contractor running most of the food-service operation, with a smattering of subcontractors, was reversed, with the subs as a group holding the contract. In most cities, this food-court model has created more food-service revenue, and its participants have grown other locations in their expanded business. The localized menu items were now at the airports.

• ● •

Collaborations of companies from different sectors can ban together their talents and serve new markets. Agrisoft Technologies was a teaming of farming cooperatives and a software producer. The result was a mechanism to better track farm production, crop growth, cutting schedules, harvesting, and taking products to market. This more efficient system spawned a public company and other software spin-offs to give "mom-and-pop" farmers the tools to optimally manage their small businesses.

Other coalitions of niche industry providers with software companies have initiated new products in such diverse areas as safety and security, food processing and controls, healthcare monitoring devices, environmental oversight, travel venue marketing, construction management, energy production, electronics, financial audits and compliance, and purchasing and other cost-control mechanisms.

Business Tree lesson: There are four ways to grow a business. One can sell more customers. One can cross-sell existing customers. The company can create new products and services. Fourth and most important, by partnering with others, you can create other products and services that could not exist otherwise, opening up new markets and endless opportunities.

The Statistics Tree: Business Truisms

- 70 percent of corporate CEOs think that business is too much focused on the short-term.

- 29 percent of the work force wants their boss' job.

- One out of every 12 businesses fails. Ninety percent of all e-businesses will fail.

- Ninety-eight percent of all new business starts are small businesses. Forty-five percet of small business owners are children of small business owners. And 83 percent of all domestic companies have fewer than 20 employees. Only 7 percent of all companies have 100 or more employees.

- Ninety-nine percent of all internet websites do not make a profit. Most are illustrated brochures.

- When executing strategy, 38 percent of business professionals said companies say they most need to emphasize improved profitability.

- The current success rate for organizational hires is 14 percent. If further research is put into looking at the total person and truly fitting the person to the job, then the success rate soars to 75 percent. That involves testing and more sophisticated hiring practices.

- The average person spends 150 hours each year in looking for misplaced information and files.

- The average person speaks 30,000 words per day.

- The average person is bombarded with more than 600 messages per day. More enlightened, actively communicating people are bombarded with more than 900 messages per day.

- An automobile that costs $20,000 to purchase will cost $125,000 if you total up the costs of all parts as replacements. $900 of the cost of every automobile sold goes to pay for advertising. About $516 of the cost of every new automobile is attributable to lawsuit abuse.

- The holdings of the world's libraries are doubling every 14 years.

- Thirty-five percent of Americans are involved in community service and charity activities.

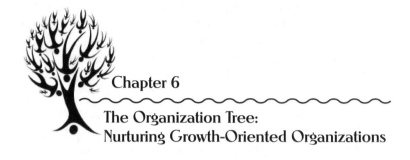

Chapter 6

The Organization Tree: Nurturing Growth-Oriented Organizations

Businesses do not start each day by focusing upon all of their dynamics in equal percentages. They usually do not get that far. It is much too easy to get bogged down with minutia. This book and my advising activities are predicated upon educating organizations on the pitfalls of narrow focus and enlightening them on the rewards of widening the view.

Will every business ever operate completely wide-scope focused? No, because vested interests and human nature want to keep attention upon the small pieces. Those organizations with the wider horizons and the most creative mosaic of the small pieces tend to stand out as the biggest successes.

People and companies make decisions based upon partial business models and the wrong information all the time. There is no reason why they cannot make new decisions based upon a widened scope of business, a fresh set of eyes, and the desire to acquire new information.

Business represents a continuing realignment of current conditions, diced with opportunities. Masterpieces are continually evolving works in progress.

The successful organization develops and champions the tools for change. The quest is to manage change, rather than to fall victim of it. This chapter includes organizational cycles and what full-scope planning could encompass, per each branch on the Business Tree. Guidelines are offered for the process of growth oriented planning.

A content outline for a strategic plan, with major headings, is included. This chapter discusses levels of planning that may be utilized by organizations and the basics of company growth realities that must be reflected in the planning process.

Every business, corporation, entrepreneurship, professional association, and non-profit organization goes through cycles in its lifetime. To assume that definitive cycles do not occur is to bury one's head in the sand. To predict and predate the cycles means greater success, earlier than fate would have it.

At any point, each organization is in a different phase from others in its industry. The astute organization assesses the status of each program and orients its team members to meet constant change and fluctuation. Phases in the life cycle of every organization include:

1. Conception. A great idea is born, and everyone is off and running.

2. Birth. The decision is made to form a company to take that idea to fruition.

3. Childhood. The organization starts to swell, and its people learn the ropes.

4. Youth. Through trial and error, a slow, steady growth occurs.

5. Maturity. The organization reaches its stride.

6. Stagnation. The bureaucratic mindset has taken over. Running an entity is more important than remaining consistent to the company vision, which may have never existed or been developed.

7. Decline. Losses abound in terms of people, processes, market share, and enthusiasm. This is a signal to take actions to rejuvenate the enthusiasm and, hopefully, to launch a new growth curve in the company's next era.

8. Death. There simply is no use for the dead organization any longer. It has played out, outlived its usefulness, and cannot come back in some other business capacity.

In business, position number eight is not an option, and strategic planning should not wait until position seven (decline) before embarking upon the process. The best time to regularly implement strategic planning programs is at every stage, numbers one through five. If your company develops strategies continually, then stagnation will rarely ever occur, and the organization will avoid going into a decline.

Guidelines for Planning the Company's Future

Strategic planning is not something that happens once and for all. Leadership should examine their organization's strategy and initiate—and periodically re-initiate—the process when any of the following conditions exist:

1. There seems to be a need to change the direction of the organization.

2. There is a need to step up growth and improve profitability.

3. There is a need to develop better information to help management make better decisions.

4. Management is concerned that resources are not concentrated on important things.

5. Management expresses a need for better internal coordination of company activities.

6. The environment in which the organization competes is rapidly changing.

7. There is a sense that company operations are out of control.

8. Management of the organization seems tired or complacent.

9. Management is cautious and uncertain about the company's future.

10. Individual managers are more concerned about their own areas than for the overall health of the organization.

Strategic planning fulfills a variety of practical and useful purposes. It constitutes disciplined thinking about the organization, its environment, and its future. It facilitates the identification of conflicts in perspective. It provides the reinforcement of team building and cohesion. It is a vehicle for monitoring organizational progress.

Strategic planning is a road map for company growth and progress. In order to be an effective process, the plan must be measurable, motivating, realistic, holistic, and consistent with the culture of the organization. Because most organizations do not have corporate cultures, this process tends to evolve one or change a culture that has evolved by default.

Every strategic plan should draw upon the organization's history. Depending upon the nature of the company, it should be two to five years in duration, with revisions annually. Realistic plans must contain attainable goals that can be measured for success. The writing of the plan should involve as many people in the organization as possible, representing each branch of the tree.

Many events and circumstances cause an organization to realize that a comprehensive look at its future is essential to avoid past pitfalls. At this crossroads, seven strategic questions must be asked of the organization:

1. Do you have financial projections for the next year in writing?
2. Do you have goals for the next year in writing?
3. Are the long-range strategic planning and budgeting processes integrated?
4. Are planning activities consolidated into a written organizational plan?
5. Do you have a written analysis of organizational strengths and weaknesses?
6. Do detailed action plans support each major strategy?
7. Do you have a detailed, written analysis of your market area?

Differentiation should now be made of the different kinds of planning processes that businesses utilize. Many refer to one when they are thinking of or actually needing another. Though none of these can substitute for a strategic plan, each is a component of the larger, more holistic future projection process.

A business plan is a front-end document, enough to get initial financing. An operational plan addresses facilities, policies, and procedures. Sales and marketing plans address business development.

If one believes vendors and niche consultants, the definition of growth strategies are what their specialty is. It may be human resources organization, training, technology, health and wellness, sales, marketing, advertising, public relations, core business, or life coaching. Few of those consultants have written full-scope strategic plans and do not really comprehend what the visioning process actually is.

Steps in the Strategic Planning Process

An effective strategic plan may be developed in a couple of months for small organizations. For mid-sized companies, it takes three or four months because performance reviews of programs must be accomplished, and further time is necessary for studies of trends and marketplaces. Large corporations devote nine months to the process because it entails holding many meetings. The planning process becomes a "campaign" in the organization, with status updates, receptions to call attention to progress, and celebrations of accomplishments. It is a long process but seeks to build cohesion in oversized organizations, attempting to amass buy-in at each step along the way.

In each case, assemble a team of thought leaders. Ask each to write down their ideas, and set an agenda to keep the process on track and on time.

Although every strategic planning process is uniquely designed to fit the specific needs of a particular organization, every successful model includes most of these steps.

Vision

A clear and realistic identification of the organization's vision and mission is the first step of any strategic planning process. The vision sets out the reasons for organization's existence and the ideal state that it aims to achieve.

Most companies need to review their original vision. By recalling the wider-scope thinking that created the company, then this new strategic planning process is consistent with original intentions, with newer processes and further benchmarks added.

Mission

The mission identifies major goals and performance objectives. Both are defined within the framework of the organizations philosophy and are used as a context for development and evaluation of intended and emergent strategies.

I cannot overemphasize the importance of a clear vision and mission. None of the subsequent steps will matter if the organization is not certain where it is headed.

The mission statement is usually the last element to be updated, after other aspects of the plan unfold. It can be grand, but it cannot be pompous. It must be pertinent and achievable.

Here are some examples of mission statements:

> TRANSCENDENT TECHNOLOGIES will exemplify professionalism in scope for emerging entrepreneurial industries...focusing its efforts toward identifying and filling niches for high quality programs, direct services, and high standards of business collaboration.

> HIGHLAND VILLAGE will help tenants to grow and prosper by providing professional shopping center management, showcasing a quality specialty retailing environment, stimulating merchant collaborations, and inspiring marketing direction... toward the ultimate benefit of customers.

> THE CHILD CARE COUNCIL will administer high-quality programs, training, and support services for the benefit of children and families in all strata of the greater metropolitan area...fulfilling niches for information and referral, direct services, and community stewardship.

Goals

Effectiveness is defined as the increase in value of people and their activities as resources. Because standards are spelled out, one knows what is expected. The main reason why people do not perform is that they do not know what is expected of them. Through goal setting and achievement, one becomes actualized. With goals, one can be a winner. Without goals, one merely averts-survives the latest crisis.

Objectives

Use indicators and indices wherever they can be used. Use common indicators where categories are similar, and use special indicators for special jobs. Let your people participate in devising the indicators. Make all indicators meaningful, and retest them periodically. Use past results as only one indicator for the future. Have a reason for setting all indicators in place. Indicators are not ends in themselves, only a means of getting where the organization needs to go. Indicators must promote actions.

Objectives under one's own responsibility help one to identify with the objectives of the larger organization of which he/she is a part. A sense of belonging is enhanced.

Achieving goals that one set and to which one commits enhances a person's sense of adequacy. People who set and are striving to achieve goals together have a sense of belonging, a major motivator for humanity.

Tactics

This is the section of the strategic plan where the action is. Having broad vision and lofty goals is the wider-scope perspective. Then, each objective must be measured to each goal. Objectives must then be delineated by tactics. Put simply, tactics spell out who is responsible for what activities, on what time lines, and according to which prerequisites. Thereafter, all benchmarks of success will be judged against specific tactics and how they fit into goals and objectives.

Environmental Scan

Once the vision and mission are clearly identified, the organization must analyze its external and internal environment. The environmental scan analyzes information about the organization's external environment (economic, social, demographic, political, legal, technological, and international factors), the industry, and internal organizational factors.

SWOT Analysis: Strengths, Weaknesses, Opportunities, and Threats

This is a comprehensive look at the organization's own situation. It candidly addresses real and perceived issues. Usually, as the process moves forward, companies are relieved to see that concepts they may have felt were problematic are actually opportunities in disguise. They see that the strengths and opportunities far outweigh the weaknesses. Armed with these insights, the strategic plan becomes more specific in addressing circumstances. It also addresses problems of marketplaces in which the company must participate.

Gap Analysis

Organizations evaluate the difference between their current position and their desired future through gap analysis. As a result, an organization can develop specific strategies and allocate resources to close the gap and achieve desired new objectives.

Benchmarking

Measuring and comparing the organization's operations, practices, and performance against others is useful for identifying "best" practices. Through an ongoing systematic benchmarking process, organizations find a reference point for setting their own goals and targets.

These are realities of a healthy benchmarking mentality:

- Some facets of the company will be proven to be working well. Others inevitably will have exhibited room for improvement.

- Successfully benchmarked companies cannot become defensive.

- The goal is to help the organization improve overall.

- Inevitably, there will be comparisons. The defensiveness of studied operating managers comes from their pride and from a sense that benchmarking is to render judgment on their management proficiency. That is not the point.

- If one's benchmarking partners are chosen carefully, they will out-perform the overall organization.

- It is fine to defend a good operation. It is a sign of strength to admit shortcomings and be the hero in bolstering certain units.

- The best benchmarked departments are eager to learn from others.

- Benchmarked companies take pride in adapting the processes so that they will work better. Thus, they don't have to reinvent what somebody did elsewhere. They adapt, rather than adopt.

- Great benchmarkers resist the tendency for this to become a beauty contest.

It is too easy to claim a number-one ranking or avoid the embarrassment of a poor ranking. It is vital to view continuous quality improvement in sportsmanship terms: all for one and one for all.

The most common benchmarking mistakes are that internal processes are unexamined, that site visits "feel good" but do not elicit substantive data or ideas, and that questions and goals are vague. The effort is too broad or has too many parameters. The focus is general and not upon actual processes. The team is not fully committed to the effort. Homework and/or advanced research is not assigned and conducted, and the wrong subjects for benchmarking are selected. Other mistakes include failing to look outside its own organization and industry and where no follow-up action is taken.

Strategic Issues

The organization determines its strategic issues based upon and consistent with its vision and mission, and within the framework of environmental and other analyses. Strategic issues are the fundamental issues the organization has to address to achieve its mission and move toward its desired future.

Strategic Programming

It is necessary to address strategic issues and develop deliberate strategies for achieving their mission. Organizations set strategic goals, action plans, and tactics during the strategic programming stage. Strategic goals are the milestones the organization aims to achieve that evolve from the strategic issues. The goals are specific, measurable, agreed upon, realistic, and time/cost bound. Action plans define how the organization gets to where it needs to go and the steps required to reach strategic goals. Tactics are specific actions used to achieve the strategic goals and implement the strategic plans.

Emergent Strategies

Unpredicted and unintended events frequently occur that differ from the organization's intended strategies, and it must respond. Emergent strategy is a consistency of behavior through time, a realized situation that was not expressly intended in the original planning of strategy. It results from a series of actions converging into a consistent pattern.

Evaluation of Individual Strategies

Periodic reviews of strategies, tactics, and action programs are essential to the success of the strategic planning process. It is important to measure performance at least annually (but preferably every quarter) to evaluate the effect of specific actions on long-term results and on the organization's vision and mission. The organization should measure current performance against previously set expectations and consider any changes or events that may have impacted the desired course of actions.

Review of the Strategic Plan

After assessing the progress of the strategic planning process, the organization needs to review the plan itself, making necessary changes and adjusting its course based upon these evaluations. The revised plan must take into consideration emergent strategies and changes affecting the organization's intended course.

Thinking More Strategically, More Consistently

With time, people in the organization routinely make their decisions within the framework of the organization's strategic vision and plan. Strategic planning becomes an organizational norm, deeply embedded within the organization's decision-making process, and participants learn to think strategically as part of their regular daily activities. Strategic thinking involves analyzing options against a range of alternatives and decisions that will chart the organization's future course.

Elements of a Full Strategic Plan

Mission Statement—Why we are in operation.

Vision—What we want to become. It fulfills the mission.

Goals—Broad statements of direction.

Objectives (what we wish to accomplish, with **Specific Tactics** attached (action steps required in order to reach each objective):

1. Core business-services.
2. Administrative.
3. Financial.
4. People, Staff development.

5. Promotional, Marketing, Customer service.
6. Quality.
7. Planning, Visioning for the organization's future.

Organizational Values:
1. Internal.
2. External.

Strengths.

Weaknesses.

Opportunities.

Threats.

Priority Issues.

Trend Analyses:
1. The environment in which business is conducted.
2. Market for retaining customer-stakeholder base.
3. Market for adding stakeholders.
4. Market for expansion of core business.
5. Competitive situation with other organizations.
6. Demographics of the professions, companies, and principal players.
7. Factors of the economy.
8. Regulator-public sector issues, challenges, and opportunities.
9. Technology issues.
10. Factors surrounding service delivery.
11. Collaborations, partnering, and joint venturing with other organizations.

Strategy Formulations.

Finance.

Human Resources:
1. Organizational chart.
2. Job descriptions, Staff.
3. Job descriptions, Board.

Resource Allocation.

Benchmarks, Measurements.

Follow-up Processes, Performance Reviews.

Business Tree Departmental Headings Within a Strategic Plan

Branch 1: Core Business

Establishing points of difference, overcome misperceptions, and own niche segments.

Development and sophistication of current programs-services.

Roles, responsibilities, and functions for each contributor to programs.

Recognizing and demanding quality in work output.

Diversification of programs-services.

Learning new industries.

Branch 2: Running the Business

Divisionalization of activities, processes, and procedures.

Time management, just-in-time delivery, and other business-accepted efficiencies.

Accomplishing the greatest possible efficiencies, results, and objectives.

Branch 3: Financial

Fiduciary responsibility.

Funding activities.

Portfolio planning.

Relationships with funding sources.

Exploring new streams of revenue.

Financial and technological resources.

Accountability to all stakeholders.

Branch 4: People

Diversity is the fundamental thread that makes the organization successful.

Human resources, staffing the programs.

Training for service providers, associates, and employees.

Team-building.

Ongoing professional development and mentoring each other.

Cross-applying talents and experiences from one program to the other.

Branch 5: Business Development

Selling and marketing the organization to desired constituencies.

Development of community contacts and resources.

Category 6: Body of Knowledge, the Organization's Long-Term Goals

Taking focus of trends, challenges, and opportunities.

Corporate culture adjustment, evolving into corporate mindset.

Collaborations, joint venturing, and partnering.

Quality improvement processes.

Developing and maintaining benchmarks for quality assurance and compliance.

Category 7: Planning for the Future
Ultimate evolution into new strata of service delivery.

Strategic planning for the entire organization.

Utilizing, learning from, and benefiting from previous planning efforts.

Linkage of benefits from planned, orderly growth.

Holding retreats to review and fine-tune the plan and strategies.

Keeping focus in relation to where the organization is headed long-term.

Planning and Goal-Setting in Downsized Times

The role for strategic planning and visioning is the highest that it has ever been. Resources are down. This condition is permanent. The situation will begin to feel normal soon.

Just as companies must have cohesive plans, so must each branch on the Business Tree, meaning each function and department. Professionals must focus upon what you achieve, not what you do. Know your mission (ends and means). Be ruthless about cost control. Be obsessive about quality. Find newer, quicker, and simpler ways to do what you do. Manage the company better by accomplishing goals and objectives. Improve people management. Use allies and their resources by collaborating with other companies and professionals. Hire over-achievers.

Identify business goals and work on the desired or requested goals exclusively. Challenge every program element to achieve goals. Empower staff to achieve business results. Define everyone's job commensurate to goals that relate back to a biog picture of the company, not just as a series of tasks.

Measure the right things, such as business issues and behavior changes. Management must know, understand, and agree to the indicators. Those who utilize strategic planning are the proprietors of the scorecard, focusing upon available funding.

Getting the resources that you need from tight-fisted management is an ongoing process. Cash outlays are justifiable either by dollars they bring in or dollars they stand to save for the organization. Cash outlays are always risks. Justify your risks in proportion to activities they have previously funded. Validate your worth to the overall company operation.

Corporate management has three alternatives for funding every department: those they must fund, those they may or may not fund, and those they will not fund. The three horsemen of funding are: how much, how soon, and how sure.

These are ways for each branch (department) in an organization to advance your funding process. Put money in management's pockets. Get to the front of the line for funding requests. Acquire an upper-management mindset. Condense the funding cycle. Become top management's partner in the efficiency and accountability of operations.

In order to get departmental planning accepted more readily, demonstrate your commitment toward strategic planning. Know, refine, and control your branch values. Take ownership of company values. Continue raising the bar on values.

In making the case for funding of further planning, link it to strategic business objectives. Diagnose a competitively disadvantaging problem or an unrealized opportunity for competitive advantage. Prescribe a more competitively advantaged outcome. Predict the benefits of the improved cash flows and diagram the improved work flows that contribute to them. Team the project. Maintain accountability and communications toward top management. Contribute to the organization's big picture.

Demons That Thwart Strategic Planning	
Dealing with problematic behaviors.	Marketing hype for the status quo.
Dysfunctional strategies.	Addictions to not trying.
Little or no work ethic.	Addictiveness to band-aid surgery.
Working without benchmarks.	Fear.
Blunders, cover-ups, and excuses.	Abdicating too easily to others' values.
Mediocrity. Complacency.	Ignorance.
Looking too much inward.	Not seeing the warning signs.
False sense of security.	Believing the hype.
Myths, hype, and over-generalizations.	The "what's hot right now" syndrome.
Addictions to failing.	Fear of success.

Reasons Why Management Supports Planning

There are three categories of attitudes of management toward planning. The **reactive** mode is dedicated toward undoing changes that have occurred. The **inactive** mode is predicated upon preventing change. The third and best mode is **proactive**, which thrives upon accelerating change.

Proactive management sees planning as adapting optimally to trends, events, and challenges. Departmental planning within the strategic plan is all about seizing opportunities, incentives, responsiveness, inducing cooperation, reducing conflict, and using conflicting ideas to generate new alternatives and countermeasures. Departments wind up advocating further future-based planning and visioning.

Human beings live to attract goals. Organizations get people caught in activity traps, unless managers periodically pull back and reassess in terms of goals. Managers often can lose sight of their employees' goals. Staff caught in activity traps shrink, rather than grow, as human beings.

Hard work that only succeeds in producing failures will tend to yield apathy, inertia, and loss of self-esteem. People become demeaned or diminished as human beings when their work proves meaningless. Realistic goals can curb this from happening.

Discipline at work is accepted, for the most part, voluntarily. If not voluntarily accepted, it is not legitimate. Discipline is a shaper of behavior, not a punishment. The past provides useful insights into behavior, but it is not the only criteria to be used.

Failure can stem from either non-achievement of goals or never knowing what they were. The tragedy is both economic and humanistic. Unclear objectives produce more failures than incompetence, bad work, bad luck, or misdirected work.

When people know and have helped set their goals, their performance improves. The best motivator is knowing what is expected and analyzing one's performance relative to mutually agreed-upon criteria.

Goal attainment leads to ethical behavior. The more an organization is worth, the more worthy it becomes. Most management subsystems succeed or fail according to the clarity of goals of the overall organization.

To make goal setting a reality, start at the top to adopt a policy of strategic planning. Goals and objectives must filter downward throughout the organization. Training on goal achievement for staff is vital. Continual follow-up, refinement, and new goal setting must ensue. Programs must be competent, effective, and benchmarked. A corporate culture must foster all goal setting, policies, practices, and procedures.

Cliches and Terms That Do NOT Belong in Strategic Planning and Corporate Strategy:

Solutions	World class	Good to go
The brand	Hearts and minds	Customer experience
Technology	The end of the day	Results
Value proposition	Virtual	Perfection
Perfection	Easy	Capitalism
Number one	Better, best	Cool
Sales leader	For all your needs	Best in breed
Customer care	Handle problems	Game changing
Learning organization	Do the math	

These expressions are trite, are meaningless, and reflect a copycat way of thinking.

Solutions is a tired 1990s term, taken from technology hype. People who use it are vendors, selling what they have to solve your "problems," rather than diagnosing and providing what your company needs. It is a misnomer to think that a quick fix pawned off as a "solution" will take care of a problem once and for all. Such a word does not belong in conversation and business strategy, let alone the name of the company.

Street talk, misleading slogans, and terms taken out of context do not belong in the business vocabulary. Business planning requires insightful thinking and language that will clearly delineate what the company mission is and how it will grow.

Dynamics and Benefits of Strategic Planning

In strategic planning for emerging industries, the company must define itself as either a first-mover or latecomer. First-mover advantages include industry leadership, brand name, entrance barrier, and the position of being a standard setter. Latecomer strategies take a "wait and then invest" attitude, embracing cost leadership and imitation. Expect to see new entrants with the advent of new or improved technologies.

In growing industries, such as healthcare, the technologies are being standardized. There is already a large established market, with customer acceptance of products. Industry winners emerge, and well-financed new entrants seek pieces of the marketplace.

Strategic planning for growth industries means expanding the domestic and international markets aggressively. There are increased economies of scope. Planning helps establish industry standards, fending off newcomers by managing value-chains and globalization strategy.

Maturing industries have saturated markets and slow growth. There are many competitors. Competition drives down price, which translates to low profit margins. Long-time customers tend to be sophisticated and demanding. The technology is mature. Process-based competition drives production costs. There is much industrial consolidation, with opportunities for mergers and acquisitions.

Strategic planning for maturing industries focuses upon cost leadership, process-driven competition, and scale economy. The plan looks to streamline product lines, acquire or eliminate rival firms, look for new technologies or products, and look toward new markets.

There are seven levels of planning that may be utilized by organizations, paralleling Business Tree branches:

1. **Information-Gathering Process.** Also known as pre-planning research, this is a snapshot of the realities, situations, facts, figures, and truths.

2. **Studying How the Organization Operates.** These insights occur during the conducting of performance reviews of successful activities, while also looking for efficiencies.

3. **Financial.** Strategic companies must enhance efficiencies, economies, and profitability, focusing upon the company's impact upon shareholder value.

4. **Process for and About Teams.** In large organizations, the planning and visioning processes become big events. Subsequent meetings and activities are orchestrated in such a way as to empower and involve the organization's most valuable resource: its people.

5. **Business Development.** In adapting to changing marketplaces and business relationships, the organization connects beliefs with expertise. Actions are taken with measurements of success and accountability toward the company's stakeholders.

6. **Strategic Planning.** This important process enables the organization to study and refine its core values. The company that possesses commitment, ownership, and the ability to change and adapt will survive the tough times and stay successful longer.

7. **Focus Upon Change and Growth.** At this level, the organization is highly sophisticated in conducting the strategic planning process. Everything is done based upon beliefs and systems of thought. The company's leaders and employees are all committed to and thrive upon change.

Markets always seek new and more profitable customer bases. Planning must prepare for crises, profit from change, and benchmark the progress. "More of the same" is not a growth strategy, nor is someone's pet agenda or other excuses for successful business.

Corporate strategies are formed through productive strategic planning. Hewlett-Packard started as a maker of printing technology. Its planning took it into computer production and ancillary technology products. Its consulting division (Agilent Technologies) evolved when the company roots indicated a new tree could nurture new forms of business. AT&T spun off its "baby bells" after the telecommunications industry deregulation. The resulting companies grew by acquiring and bundling new technologies, such as cell phones, only years later rolling back up as AT&T. These growths are all attributable to thoughtful strategic planning processes by those corporations.

These are some successful corporate strategies that I was not a part of advising, though I salute what they did. Trans Texas Airways evolved to the next tier as Southwest Airlines, based upon strong customer service and traveler loyalty components. The Build-a-Bear Workshop and Starbuck's chains represent the next generation of franchises, where positive lifestyle and congeniality are the core business.

The Pokemon phenomenon could be considered multicultural and multi-media play. As a grandfather, we watch a lot of Pokemon videos and see the cards and, thus, company philosophy as promoting teamwork and youthful empowerment. Future entertainment and franchising enterprises will benefit from strategy driven companies that created new marketplaces, which created further strategic intent for growth. The planning and idea processes are very cylindrical.

Success Rates for Strategic Planning

Done in a vacuum, without top-down support:

One person writes it for the unit-company and presents.	18%
CEO creates it and pressures executives and staff to support.	23%
Internal team devises the plan and presents for approval.	27%
Non-qualified advisor writes (perhaps as part of an audit).	29%
Qualified external advisor writes the plan, and executives later adopt.	53%
Combination of team with advisor develop the plan.	64%

Done with full top-down support and management encouragement:

One person writes it for the unit-company and presents.	31%
CEO creates it and pressures executives and staff to support.	39%
Internal team devises the plan and presents for approval.	58%
Non-qualified advisor writes (perhaps as part of an audit).	47%
Qualified external advisor writes the plan, and executives later adopt.	53%
Combination of team with qualified advisor develop the plan.	85%
Combined with Corporate Visioning and departmental plans.	94%

Making the Process Work

There are three kinds of people in business: those who make things happen, those who watch, and those who don't know what hit them. Understand the differences, among your team, customer base, competition, and referral sources.

Know the business you're really in. Prioritize the actual reasons why you provide services, what customers want, and external influences. Where all three intersect constitutes the growth strategy.

Focus more upon service and less on hype. Dispel the widely held expectations of poor customer service. Building relationships is paramount to adding, holding, and getting referrals for further business.

Every branch on your Business Tree must possess commitment and ownership. Plans do not work unless they consider input and practicalities from those who will carry them out. Know the people involved, and develop their leadership abilities.

Here are my recommended guidelines for conducting strategic planning for any organization:

- Utilize outside consultants. Do not conduct all of the planning internally. Keep objectivity.

- Allow sufficient time for this process to succeed.

- Keep the procedure simple and disciplined.

- Develop the plan in stages.

- Set specific objectives.

- Set operating policies from the planning document.

- Ensure that the plan meets organizational needs.

- Find and keep champions for your forward-moving process.

- Involve those who will implement the plan in developing it.

- Do not spread your resources too thinly.

- Communicate the results of the process to all affected parties.

- Tailor the actions toward the organization's true culture.

- Be willing to change as the process matures.

- Be open minded.

- Apply feedback to the continuing planning process.

- Keep the plan alive.

The ultimate benefits of strategic planning include enhanced problem prevention capabilities of the organization. Group-based strategic decisions reflect the best available alternatives. Team motivation should be enhanced. Gaps and overlaps in activities should reduce. Resistance to change should be reduced.

No company can solely focus inward. Understand forces outside your company that can drastically alter plans and adapt strategies accordingly.

Evaluate things you really can do. Overcome the "nothing works" cynicism via partnerships and long-range problem-solving. It requires more than traditional or short-term measures. He who upsets something should know how to rearrange it. Anyone can poke holes at organizations. The valuable leaders know the processes of pro-active change, implementation, and benchmarking the achievements.

Take a holistic approach to individual and corporate development. Band-aid surgery only perpetuates problems. Focus upon substance, rather than "flash and sizzle." Success is incrementally attained, and then the yardstick is pushed progressively higher.

● ● ●

What Motivates People to Work and Achieve
(per each category of the Business Tree)

Branch 1: The Business You're In

Doing good work, with standards of professionalism.

Producing products/services that make a difference.

Branch 2: Running the Business

Maintaining high productivity.

Ability to control and influence.

Making correct decisions.

Branch 3: Financial

Receiving adequate compensation.

Maintain standards of accountability.

Branch 4: People

Being accepted and acknowledged.

Being part of a motivated team.

Receiving praise, recognition, and advancement.

Having a certain amount of freedom on the job.

Learning new things.

Enjoying work relationships and having fun with the job.

Achieving balance in life, thus becoming a more
valuable employee.

Working with good managers and leaders.

Being perceived as a role model.

Branch 5: Business Development

Direct involvement in important projects.

Doing work that empowers customers.

Integrity, with customers and ourselves.

Category 6: Body of Knowledge

Exemplifying standards of quality.

Remaining confident about work.

Exemplifying value and excellence.

Need for personal and professional growth.

Category 7: The Big Picture

Feeling like you've made a positive contribution.

Accomplishing worthwhile things.

Being in an organization that makes a difference.

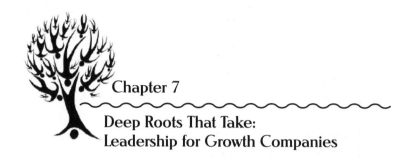

Chapter 7

Deep Roots That Take:
Leadership for Growth Companies

Developing the Right Talent to Reach the Next Level

It's lonely at the top. Corporate executives must develop themselves for the next level and to be useful to their companies and communities in the future.

This chapter is a primer for executives and the heirs apparent to company leadership. Critical topics include leadership development of executives, mindset changes in the evolution from manager to executive to leader, executive mentoring, insights into how top professionals evolve, plateaus of professional accomplishment, developing a winning work ethic, life-long learning, and the accrual of business wisdom.

Many books have been written on the subject of leadership. They came from training, team-building, and similar Branch 4 perspectives. This book sees the leader from the big-picture perspective and how he/she paints career panoramas by interconnecting the pieces.

My own philosophy of leadership starts with the premise that every dynamic of a successful organization must be in some way aimed toward its stakeholders. Although all good leaders must keep the company's internal operations moving forward, the very best ones must also be looking outside the company toward the customers, clients, financiers, and volunteers, and the organization's entire affected constituencies. If management is complacent or is not outward-looking, then the same attitude and resulting behaviors will be held by employees who render the services. Failure to keep a clear focus upon the product, its marketplace, its customers, and the people who influence the company's ultimate success will eventually do great harm to the company.

I believe that a good leader is also a community leader. I once advised a U.S. president in fostering the Thousand Points of Light program, a national effort to spur volunteerism, hope, and good works throughout the country, and will draw upon lessons learned from that program.

Most companies want and need to give back to the communities in which they do business. The most successful ones realize that everyone wins by such activities. They also know that executives who serve on community boards will improve their leadership skills through the process, thus making them more valuable to the company. By recognizing and praising corporate organizations, entrepreneurs, and company rising stars, they will try even harder to do better. Community stewardship programs are opportunities for involvement, achievement, and commitment to the wider scope of business.

The Management Tree: How and Why Leadership Styles Sprout

Branch 1: The Business You're In: You are not just in the widget business (as a symbol for core business). You're in the business of making, processing, financing, empowering, selling, researching, marketing, benchmarking, administering, and facilitating widgets to your customer base. Without thinking and acting beyond Branch 1, you have no business in which to make your widgets.

Branch 2: **Running the Business:** In assessing company operations, three rights offset a wrong. There is much more right about your organization than you might think. Recognize and salute strengths as such, rather than categorize them as weaknesses.

Branch 3: **Financial:** Just as widget creation (core business niche) constitutes 10 percent, please keep financial aspects in comparable perspective.

Branch 4: **People:** There's a big difference between experience and expertise. Training bridges the differences. Without empowering your people, you will not recognize full organizational potential. They must work *with* you, not *for* or *against* you. The more that people see what's in it for them (other than a paycheck), they will support and embody company goals, knowing that other people care.

Branch 5: **Business Development:** Unless you're selling something, you're not in business. Growing a business isn't just a factor of selling more.

Category 6 (trunk): **Body of Knowledge:** When the organization stops learning, it is on the road to failure. Niche specialists look through their perspective, not through the full organizational lens. Leadership must view the business as a whole.

Category 7 (roots): **The Big Picture:** The best leaders bring out the sense of visionary in the management team and develop the next generation of leaders with the widest possible perspective.

Grounds and Turf: Leadership Realities for Your Tree

Not all executives are leaders. Not all managers are executives. Not all career people are professional.

Top company management usually comes from the ranks of those who sell the core business product-service, not from those on the firing line who deliver it. That's why in media, programming, and news people rarely become management. Because advertising sales is the primary product of media, the salespeople become the managers. In education, good teachers stay in the classroom. In the energy industry, engineers dominate. Engineers steadfastly believe that they're in the energy exploration and production business. The companies themselves are in the energy marketing business.

Restaurants are in the business of marketing atmosphere and service. Yet, they put food preparers (representing 20 percent of the pie) in charge. Decisions are always food-driven, explaining in part the high failure rate of restaurants. Other reasons include poor planning, substandard customer service, low capitalization, and inappropriate marketing.

A major problem with companies stems from the fact that management and company leadership come from one small piece of the organizational pie. Filling all management slots with financial people, for example, serves to limit the organizational strategy and focus. They all hire like-minded people and frame every business decision from their micro-perspective.

The ideal executive has strong leadership skills first. He/she develops organizational vision and sets strategies. Leaders should reflect a diversity of focus, guaranteeing that a balance is achieved. The best management team looks at the macro, rather than just the niche micro.

None of us was born with sophisticated, finely tuned senses and highly enlightened viewpoints for life. We muddle through, try our best, and get hit in the gut several times. Thus, we learn, amass knowledge, and turn most experiences into strategies. Such a perspective is what makes seasoned executives valuable in the business marketplace.

Life has a way of forcing the human condition to change. Events that may inspire this to happen could include a recognition that the old methods are not working, financial failures, or the monetary incentive to rapidly create or change plans of action. At most crossroads, there is no choice but to change the modus operandi. This may include the loss of substantial numbers of opportunities, customers, employees, and market share, or a wake-up call of any type.

The most effective leaders accept that change is 90-percent positive, and find reasons and rationale to embrace change. Leadership skills are learned and synthesized daily. Knowledge is usually amassed through unexpected sources.

Management Styles

In the period that predated scientific management, the Captain of Industry style prevailed. Prior to 1885, the kings of industry were rulers, as had been land barons of earlier years. Policies were dictated, and people complied. Some captains were notoriously ruthless. Others, like Rockefeller, Carnegie, and Ford, channeled their wealth and power into giving back to the communities. It was an era of self-made millionaires and the people who toiled in their mills.

From 1885 to 1910, the labor movement gathered steam. Negotiations and collective bargaining focused on conditions for workers and physical plant environments. In this era, business fully segued from an agricultural-based economy to an industrial-based reality.

As a counterbalance to industrial reforms and the strength of unions, a Hard-Nosed style of leadership was prominent from 1910 to 1939. This was management's attempt to take stronger hands, recapture some of the Captain of Industry style, and build solidity into an economy plagued by the Depression. This is an important phase to remember because it is the mind-set of addictive organizations.

The Human Relations style of management flourished from 1940 to 1964. Under it, people were managed. Processes were managed as collections of people. Employees began having greater says in the execution of policies. Yet, the rank-and-file employees at this point were not involved in creating policies, least of all strategies and methodologies.

Management by Objectives came into vogue in 1965 and was the prevailing leadership style until 1990. In this era, business started embracing formal planning. Other important components of business (training, marketing, research, team-building, and productivity) were all accomplished according to goals, objectives, and tactics.

In 1991, Customer-Focused Management became the standard. It will be discussed at length in this chapter.

Most corporate leaders are two management styles behind. Those who matured in the era of the Human Relations style of management were still clinging to value systems of Hard-Nosed. They were not just "old school"; they went to the school that was torn down to build the old school.

Executives who were educated in the Management by Objectives era were still recalling value systems of their parents' generation before it. Baby Boomers with a Depression-era frugality and value of tight resources are more likely to take a bean counter–focused approach to business. That's my concern: that financial-only focus without regard to other corporate dynamics bespeaks of hostile takeovers, ill-advised rollups, and corporate raider activity in search of acquiring existing books of business.

To follow through the premise, younger executives who were educated and came of age during the early years of Customer-Focused Management had still not comprehended and embraced its tenets. As a result, the dotcom bust and subsequent financial scandals occurred. In a nutshell, the "new school" of managers did not think that corporate protocols and strategies related to them. The game was to just write the rules as they rolled along. Such thinking always invites disaster, as so many of their stockholders found out. Given that various management eras are still reflected in the new order of business, we must learn from each and move forward.

Potlache

Potlache is the ultimate catalyst toward Customer-Focused Management. It means extra gifts, beyond value-added, visionary mindset, and the ultimate achievement of the organization.

The word *potlache* is a Native American expression, meaning "to give." For Native Americans, the potlache was an immensely important winter ceremony featuring dancing, food, and gift giving. Potlache ceremonies were held to observe major life events. They exchanged gifts and properties to show wealth and status. Instead of the guests bringing gifts to the family, the family gave gifts to the guests.

Colonists settled and started doing things their own way, without first investigating local customs. They alienated many of the natives. Thus, the cultural differences widened. The more diverse we become, the more we really need to learn from and about others. The practice of doing so creates an understanding that spawns better loyalty.

When one gives ceremonial gifts, one gets extra value because of the spirit of the action. The more you give, the more you ultimately get back in return. Reciprocation becomes an esteemed social ceremony. It elevates the givers to higher levels of esteem in the eyes of the recipients.

Potlache is a higher level of understanding of the business that breeds loyalty and longer-term support. It leads to increased quality, better resource management, higher employee productivity, reduced operating costs, improved cash management, better management overall, and enhanced customer loyalty and retention.

The Business Leader as Community Leader

In eras following downturns and scandals, it is incumbent upon good companies to go the extra distance to be ethical and set good examples. Demonstrating visible caring for communities by company executives is the ultimate form of potlache.

No matter the size of the organization, goodwill must be banked. Every company must make deposits for those inevitable times in which withdrawals will be made.

To say that business and its communities do not affect each other is short-sighted—and will make business the loser every time. Business marries the community that it settles with. The community has to be given a reason to care for the business. Business owes its well-being and livelihood to its communities.

Business leaders have an obligation to serve on community boards and be very visible in the communities in which they do business. If done right, community stewardship builds executives into better leaders, as well as receiving deserved credit for the company. Civic service is the ultimate way to steer heir apparents toward the leadership track.

Communities are clusters of individuals, each with their own agenda. In order to be minimally successful, each company must know the components of its home community intimately. Each company has a business stake for doing its part. Community relations in reality is a function of self-interest, rather than just being a good citizen.

Companies should support off-duty involvement of employees in pro bono capacities but not take unfair credit. Volunteers are essential to community relations. Companies must show tangible evidence of supporting the community by assigning key executives to high-profile community assignments. Create a formal volunteer guild, and allow employees the latitude and creativity to contribute to the common good. Celebrate and reward their efforts.

Publicity and promotions should support effective community relations and not be the substitute or smokescreen for the process. Recognition is as desirable for the community as it is for the business. Good news shows progress and encourages others to participate.

The well-rounded community relations program embodies all elements: accessibility of company officials to citizens, participation by the company in business and civic activities, public service promotions, special events, plant communications materials and open houses, grassroots constituency building, and good citizenry.

No entity can operate without affecting or being affected by its communities. Business must behave like a guest in its communities, never failing to give potlache or return courtesies. Community acceptance of one project does not mean that the job of community relations has been completed. It is not "insurance" that can be bought overnight. It is tied to the bottom line and must be treated accordingly, with resources and expertise to do it effectively. It is a bond of trust that, if violated, will haunt the business. If steadily built, the trust can be exponentially parlayed into successful long-term business relationships.

Customer-Focused Management

In today's highly competitive business environment, every dynamic of a successful organization must be geared toward ultimate customers. Customer-Focused Management goes far beyond just smiling, answering queries, and communicating with buyers. It transcends service and quality. Every organization has customers, clients, stakeholders, financiers, volunteers, supporters, or other categories of "affected constituencies."

Companies must change their focus from products and processes to the values that they share with customers. Everyone with whom you conduct business is a customer or referral source of someone else. The service that we get from some people, we pass along to others. Customer service is a continuum of human behaviors, shared with those whom we meet.

Customers are the lifeblood of every business. Employees depend upon customers for their paychecks. Yet, you wouldn't know the correlation when poor customer service is rendered. Employees of many companies behave as though customers are a bother, do not heed their concerns, and do not take suggestions for improvement.

There is no business that cannot undergo some improvement in its customer orientation. Being the recipient of bad service elsewhere must inspire us to do better for our own customers. The more that one sees poor customer service and customer neglect in other companies, we must avoid the pitfalls and traps in our own companies.

Do you ever try to complain about poor customer service, and the total lack of empathy made you even more angry than when you contacted them in the first place? Companies tend to rationalize that lost customers are easily replaceable. Research shows that retaining 2 percent of your customers from leaving or deflecting their business has a bigger effect upon your bottom line than cutting operating costs by 10 percent.

A longtime, steady customer is three times more profitable for the business than a recently added customer. Longtime customers make referrals, which reduce the company's marketing costs. Dissatisfied customers will tell 10–20 other people.

Employees mirror management's philosophy. If they are only concerned with the cash register ringing, without giving any more, than they do not have a right to keep customers or stay in business. Those who think and behave as though customers are necessary evils and tolerate them accordingly, exemplify a mindset that decimates potlache goodwill.

If problems are handled only through form letters, subordinates, or call centers, then management is the real cause of the problem. Customer-Focused Management begins and ends at top management. Management should speak personally with customers, to set a good example for employees. If management is complacent or non-participatory, then it will be reflected by behavior and actions of the employees.

Organizations should coordinate relationship management skills into their overall corporate strategy, in order to satisfy customer needs profitably, draw together the components for practical strategies, and implement strategic requirements to impact the business.

Any company can benefit from having an advisory board, which is an objective and insightful source of sensitivity toward customer needs, interests, and concerns. The successful business must put the customer into a co-destiny relationship. Customers want to build relationships, and it is the obligation of the business to prove that it is worthy.

Customer-Focused Management is the antithesis to the traits of bad business, such as the failure to deliver what was promised, bait-and-switch advertising, and a failure to handle mistakes and complaints in a timely, equitable, and customer-friendly manner.

Don't post a Customer Service Index (CSI) rating unless you and every member of your team really know what it means. There must be a commitment to maintain it. Consumer complaints must launch a genuine action to improve. To avoid customer concerns and do business as usual is a mockery of the quality process. Such a company does not have the right to flaunt its perceived CSI rating any longer.

Customer-Focused Management is dedicated to providing members with an opportunity to identify, document, and establish best practices through benchmarking to increase value, efficiencies, and profits.

Leadership for the New Order

Within every corporate and structure, there exists a stair-step ladder. One enters the ladder at some professional level and is considered valuable for the category of services for which he/she has expertise. This ladder holds true for managers and employees within the organization, as well as outside consultants brought in.

Each professional rung on the ladder is important. At whatever level one enters the ladder, he/she should be trained, measured for performance, and fit into the organization's overall scope. This is the stair-step, paralleling the Business Tree:

1. **Resource:** One has experience with equipment, tools, materials, and schedules.

2. **Skills and Tasks:** One is concerned with activities, procedures, and project fulfillment.

3. **Role and Job:** The position is defined according to assignments, responsibilities, functions, relationships, follow-through, and accountability.

4. **Systems and Processes:** These are managers concerned with structure, hiring, control, work design, supervision, and the effects of management decisions.

5. **Strategy:** These executives spend much of their energies on planning, tactics, organizational development, and business development.

6. **Culture and Mission:** Upper management is most effective when it frames business decisions toward values, customs, beliefs, goals, objectives, and the benchmarking of tactics.

7. **Philosophy:** These are the visionaries who advise management in refining the organizational purpose, vision, quality of life, ethics, and contributions toward the company's long-term growth.

One rarely advances more than one rung on the ladder during the course of service to the organization unless he/she embodies that wider scope. The professional who succeeds the most is the one who sees himself/herself in the bigger picture and contextualizes what he/she does accordingly.

Value-added leadership is a healthy way of professional life that puts collaborations first. When all succeed, then profitability is much higher and more sustained than under the Hard-Nosed management style.

Value-added leadership requires a senior team commitment. Managers and employees begin seeing themselves as leaders and grow steadily into those roles. It is not acceptable to be a clone of what you perceive someone else to be. Those organizations and managers who use terms such as *world class* are usually wannabes who won't ever quite make the measuring stick.

Leadership means being consistently excellent and upholding standards to remain so. There is no such thing as perfection. Yet, excellence is a definitive process of achievement, dedication, and expeditious use of resources. Exponential improvement each year is the objective.

Good professionals must be role models. Leadership comes from inner quests, ethical pursuits, and professional diligence. Often, we teach others what we were never taught or what we learned the hard way. That's how this book came into being: There was no executive encyclopedia for those to make it long-term. Those who take that knowledge into practice will lead their business and industry.

If every executive devoted at least 10 percent of his/her time to these activities, then corporate scandals would not occur. Thinking and reasoning skills are not taught in school; they are amassed through a wealth of professional experiences. Planning is the thread woven through this book, and it is the key to the future. One can never review progress enough, with benchmarking being the key to implementing plans.

Many organizations fall into the trap of calling what they are doing a "tradition." That is an excuse used by many to avoid change and accountability. Just because something has been done one or two times, realize that it will get old and stale. Traditions are philosophies that are regularly fine-tuned, with elements added. Traditions are not stuck in ruts, though failing companies are.

If I could determine curriculum, every business school would require public speaking and writing courses. I'd have every professional development program devote more to leadership and thinking skills than they do to computer training. I'd also have courses with such titles as "The Business Executive as Community Leader," "Mentoring Your Own Staff," and "Role Model 101."

Management Leads in Strategically Planned Companies

Companies that are planned and have developed strategies to meet the future now subscribe to results-based management, with the goal to improve program effectiveness and accountability, and achieve results. This means that company leadership is committed to:

- Establishing clear organizational vision, mission, and priorities, which are translated into a four-year framework of goals, outputs, indicators, strategies, and resources.

- Encouraging an organizational and management culture that promotes innovation, learning, accountability, and transparency.

- Delegating authority, empowering managers, and holding them accountable for results.

- Focusing on achieving results, through strategic planning, regular monitoring of progress, evaluation of performance, and reporting on performance.

- Creating supportive mechanisms, policies, and procedures, building and improving on what is already in place.

- Sharing information and knowledge, learning lessons, and feeding these back into improving decision-making and performance.

- Optimizing human resources and building capacity among staff to manage for results.

- Making the best use of financial resources in an efficient manner to achieve results.

- Strengthening and diversifying partnerships at all levels.

- Responding to external situations and needs within the organizational mandate.

We are the products of those who believe in us. Find role models and set out to be one yourself. To get, you must give. Career and life are not a short stint. Do what it takes to run the decathlon. Set personal and professional goals, standards, and accountability.

Stand for something. Making money is not enough. You must do something worth leaving behind, mentoring to others and of recognizable substance. Your views of professionalism must be known and shown.

Mentoring and Lifelong Learning

Professionals who succeed the most are the products of mentoring. I heartily endorse that you find a great mentor.

I have had many excellent ones in my long career and have in turn mentored hundreds of others.

The mentor is a resource for business trends, societal issues, and opportunities. The mentor becomes a role model, offering insights about his/her own life-career. This reflection shows the mentee levels of thinking and perception that were not previously available. The mentor is an advocate for progress and change. Such work empowers the mentee to hear, accept, believe, and get results. The sharing of trust and ideas leads to developing business philosophies.

The mentor endorses the mentee, messages ways to approach issues, helps draw distinctions, and paints pictures of success. The mentor opens doors for the mentee. The mentor requests proactive changes of mentee, evaluates realism of goals, and offers truths about path to success and shortcomings of mentee's approaches. This is a bonded collaboration toward each other's success. The mentor stands for mentees throughout their careers and celebrates their successes. This is a lifelong dedication toward mentorship—in all aspects of one's life.

The most significant lessons that I learned in my business life from mentors, verified with experience, are shared here:

1. You cannot go through life as a carbon copy of someone else.

2. You must establish your own identity, which is a long, exacting process.

3. As you establish a unique identity, others will criticize. Being different, you become a moving target.

4. People criticize you because of what you represent, not who you are. It is rarely personal against you. Your success may bring out insecurities within others. You might be what they cannot or are not willing to become.

5. If you cannot take the dirtiest job in any company and do it yourself, then you will never become "management."

6. Approach your career as a body of work. This requires planning, purpose, and commitment. It's a career, not just a series of jobs.

7. The person who is only identified with one career accomplishment or by the identity of one company for whom he/she formerly worked is a one-hit wonder and, thus, has no body of work.

8. The management that takes steps to "fix themselves" rather than always projecting problems upon other people will have a successful organization.

9. It's not when you learn. It's that you learn.

10. Many people do without the substantive insights into business because they have not really developed critical-thinking skills.

11. Analytical and reasoning skills are extensions of critical thinking skills.

12. You perform your best work for free. How you fulfill commitments and pro-bono work speaks to the kind of professional that you are.

13. People worry so much what others think about them. If they knew how little others thought, they wouldn't worry so much. This too is your challenge: to frame how they see you and your company.

14. Fame is fleeting and artificial. The public is fickle and quick to jump on the newest flavor, without showing loyalty to the old ones, especially those who are truly original. Working in radio, I was taught, "They only care about you when you're behind the microphone."

15. The pioneer and "one of a kind" professional has a tough lot in life. It is tough to be first or so far ahead of the curve that others cannot see it. Few will understand you. Others will attain success with portions of what you did. None will do it as well.

16. Consumers are under-educated and don't know the substance of a pioneer. Our society takes more to the copycats and latest fads. Only the pioneer knows and appreciates what he/she really accomplished. That reassurance will have to be enough.

17. Life and careers include peaks and valleys. It's how one copes during the downtimes that is the true measure of success.

18. Long-term success must be earned. It is not automatic and is worthless if ill-gotten. The more dues one pays, the more you must continue paying.

19. The next best achievement is the one you're working on now, inspired by your body of knowledge to date.

20. The person who never has aggressively pursued a dream or mounted a series of achievements cannot understand the quest of one with a deeply committed dream.

21. A great percentage of the population does not achieve huge goals but still admires and learns from those who do persevere and succeed. The achiever thus becomes a lifelong mentor to others.

22. Achievement is a continuum, but it must be benchmarked and enjoyed along the way.

These are my concluding pieces of leadership advice. Know where you are going. Develop, update, and maintain a career growth document. Keep a diary of lessons learned but not soon forgotten. Learn the reasons for success and, more importantly, for failure.

Good bosses were good employees. They have keen understanding for both roles. Bad bosses likely were not ideal employees. They, too, are consistent in career history.

Being your own boss is yet another lesson. People who were downsized from a corporate environment suddenly enter the entrepreneurial world and find the transition to be tough.

Poor people skills cloud any job performance and overshadow good technical skills. The worst bosses do not sustain long careers at the top. Their track record catches up with them, whether they choose to acknowledge it or not.

Good workers don't automatically become good bosses. Just because someone is technically proficient or is an exemplary producer does not mean that he/she will transition to being a boss. The best school teachers do not want to become principals, for that reason. Good job performers are better left doing what they do best. Administrators, at all levels, need to be properly trained as such, not bumped up from the field to do something for which they have no inclination.

Truth and ethics must be woven into how you conduct business. If you do not "walk the talk," who will? Realize that very little of what happens to you in business is personal. Find common meeting grounds with colleagues. The only workable solution is a win-win.

Leadership and executive development skills are steadily learned and continually sharpened. One course or a quick-read book will not instill them. The best leaders are prepared to go the distance. Professional enrichment must be lifelong. Early formal education is but a starting point. Study trends in business, in your industry, and in the industries of your customers.

People skills mastery applies to every profession. There is no organization that does not have to communicate to others about what it does. The process of open company dialogues must be developed to address conflicts, facilitate win-win solutions, and further organizational goals.

7 Stages of a Career: Professional, Leader

1. Education-Growth. Acquiring a profession, knowledge base, and perspective.

2. Evolution. Paying substantial dues. Thinking as a manager, not as a worker.

3. Experience Gathering. Taking time in early career to steadily blossom. Being mentored by others.

4. Grooming. Sharpening people skills. Contributing to the bottom line, directly and indirectly.

5. Seasoning. Continuing to pay dues. Realizing there are no quick fixes.

6. Meaningful Contributions. Learning to expect, predict, understand, and relish success.

7. Body of Work. Acquiring perception, career durability for the long-run.

7 Plateaus of Professionalism

1. Learning and Growing. Developing resources, skills, and talents.

2. Early Accomplishments. Learning what works and why. Incorporating your own successes into the organization.

3. Professionalism. Committing to sets of standards at role, job, responsibilities and relationships. Taking stands against mediocrity, sloppiness, poor work, and low quality.

4. Commitment to Career. Enjoying successes, sharing techniques with others.

5. Seasoning. Refining career with several levels of achievement, and recognition. Learning about planning, tactics, organizational development, systems improvement.

6. Mentor-Leader-Advocate-Motivator. Developing skills in every aspect of the organization. Mentoring, creating and leading have become the primary emphasis for your career.

7. Beyond the Level of Professional. Developing and sharing a track record, contributing toward organizational philosophy, purpose, vision, quality of life, ethics, and long-term growth.

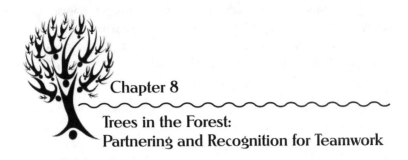

Chapter 8

Trees in the Forest:
Partnering and Recognition for Teamwork

This chapter centers upon important trends in business for future growth: collaborations, partnering, and joint venturing. It examines opportunities and strategies for these concepts.

The biggest source of growth and increased opportunities in today's business climate is in the way that individuals and companies work together. It is becoming increasingly rare to find an individual or organization that has not yet been required to team with others. Lone rangers and sole-source providers simply cannot succeed in competitive environments and global economies. Those who benefit by teaming, rather than become the victim of others, will log the biggest successes in business years ahead.

Just as empowerment, team-building, and other processes apply to employees in formal organizational structures, the teaming of independents can likewise benefit from the concepts. There are rules of protocol that support and protect partnerships, having a direct relationship to those who profit most from teaming.

Collaborations are where parties willingly cooperate, working together especially in an intellectual pursuit. They create a permanent instrumentality or third-party organization with which more than one are connected.

Here are several examples of collaborations:

Aramco formed Star Enterprise, an energy marketing organization. Shell and Texaco formed Equiva, an energy exploration and production organization. In both cases, the third-party organizations worked diligently to create their own strategic plans and corporate cultures, apart from those of the main partners.

Parties and consultants involved in taking companies public often collaborate. I have worked with law firms, accounting firms, public relations firms, manufacturing process consultants, and distribution specialists that, out of necessity, teamed up. As such, groups of consultants offer their collective talents to clients on a contract basis. This most frequently occurs with company turnaround situations, which require a multi-disciplinary approach.

Niche specialists collectively conduct research studies or performance reviews. For county governments, I put together teams with expertise germane to the departments being audited. The aggregation included a retired county judge who knew the inner-workings, a privatization consultant who had created outsourcing economies for state government, food service consultants, criminal justice professors, quality-management gurus, technology analysts, forensic accounting experts, organizational development authorities, and customer service experts. These reviews paralleled the Business Tree and yielded insights beyond the boundaries of traditional accounting firm audits. They linked directly to departmental planning and benchmarking needs.

The client needs to open new locations in new communities and ask its consultants to formulate a plan of action and oversee operating aspects. I recall mounting strategies on behalf of for-profit healthcare chains. In some cases, they acquired existing hospitals and medical practices, and in other cases it meant building facilities. The process included staging town-hall meetings and building stakeholder relationships on the front end (Branch 5). The plan then affected the challenges of competing institutions in those communities and the practicalities of acquiring other companies to be of service to this expanding chain. The team itself generated results that one or more consultants could not have achieved separately. As a result, the client organization collaborated with its communities in the further delivery of services.

The industry where the most creative opportunities exist is healthcare. Doctor-owned hospitals were originally formed when there were culture clashes with non-profit teaching hospitals. For-profit companies (more adept at business practices) took over many of the privately owned facilities. The next and current business phase is the rollup of ancillary healthcare services. The new breed of healthcare companies is a hybrid of the other institutions and must work hard to craft their own unique cultures, done so by planning and collaborating.

Storefront healthcare practices have emerged, as collaborations between medical institutions, area service providers, and community business interests. The resulting entities provide routine family healthcare services, preventive medicine projects, diet and wellness clinics, and corporate employee-assistance programs. Further collaborations involve consultants to doctors and group practices on billings, insurance company interface, collections, and doctor's office management.

The fine arts have long embraced collaborations, including composers and lyricists to write songs, film production teams, literary specialists, and more. Many of these artists of different media collaborated to create festivals, shows, and museums. Examples include Band Aid, Live Aid, USA for Africa, Farm Aid, and Hands Across America.

Other examples of collaborations include professional associations, teams of healthcare professionals, as found in clinics and hospitals, advocate groups for causes, libraries, and communities rallying around certain causes.

B usiness Tree lesson: The best collaborators have led other successful initiatives. If you've captained your own team and empowered other people to support the enterprise, then you are a more valuable member of someone else's team.

Partnering

Partnering is a formal relationship between two or more associates. This involves close cooperation among parties, with each having specified rights, roles, and responsibilities.

Partnering helps small business units accomplish more, faster than they could by themselves. The key to the process is determining when to partner and when to acquire, developing initial strategies, attracting and securing relationships, and managing and improving existing partnerships and acquisitions.

Here are some examples of partnering:

Non-competing disciplines create a new mousetrap, based upon their unique talents, and collectively pursue new marketplace opportunities. FedEx teamed with Kinko's, creating centers where customers can print documents and at the same time arrange to ship them.

Widget manufacturing companies team with retail management experts to open a string of widget stores. Disney realized that its core business was the licensing of its name and teamed with retailers to sustain the Disney stores, much in the same way that Disney partnered with Kenneth Feld Enterprises to stage the touring Disney shows.

Formal rollups or corporations provide full-scope services to customers. These often occur in the home-repairs arena, healthcare, agribusiness, technology transfer, retail malls, and large construction projects. The Associated General Contractors of America created the Apex Awards Program to recognize and promote partnering among general and specialty contractors.

Non-profit organizations often bond resources for programs or fundraising. I advised partnerships in creating umbrella agencies for such areas as literacy, daycare, family counseling, crisis hotlines, substance abuse, and senior citizen services. Not only did the umbrella agencies achieve fundraising success by their profiles with foundations, but they also conducted public awareness campaigns for their member agencies. Inevitably, the partnership umbrellas uncovered needs for additional services in their niche, and these agencies began filling the needs with newly created programs, which became the basis for further collective fundraising.

When many financial institutions provide startup or expansion capital, they insist that cooperative business practices be followed. Venture capitalists insist upon complete strategic plans for mergers, acquisitions, and divestitures, which necessitates that consultants ban together.

Examples discussed in earlier chapters included airport food courts, the Maquiladora program, city redevelopment initiatives, supply chain management, real estate development, facilities management teams, and healthcare rollups.

Other examples of partnering include retail hubs, online marketing, the creation of global markets, the development of new products, procurement and purchasing capacities, and organ-donor banks in consortium with hospitals, vendors, trainers, computer consultants, and other consultants who strategically team with clients to do business.

Just as public sector agencies and non-profit organizations base their support on partnering, there is another category called non-governmental organizations (NGOs). The biggest of the NGOs are UNICEF and CARE. I worked with both, and they are models of conviviality at putting the pieces together. UNICEF mounted Third World healthcare initiatives with the cooperation of corporate and faith-based organization partners. The Campaign for Child Survival addressed immunizations, oral re-hydration, breastfeeding, and other infant-care issues. CARE partnered with Internet companies in pioneering Empty Plate Day, the first online fundraising project.

Business Tree lesson: Carefully selected partners bring talents to the project that will grow and help other future partnerships.

Joint Venturing

Joint venturing is an arrangement where two or more parties come together for specific purposes or projects that may be beyond the scope of individual members. Each retains its own individual identity. The joint venture itself has its own identity, reflecting favorably upon work to be done and upon the partners involved. Although a lot of good business leaders are rightfully wary of unproductive joint ventures where the interests of certain participants may diverge, the joint venture remains one of the best ways for a firm or business unit to quickly expand its value network.

Here are some examples of joint venturing:

Eldercare is one of the world's fast growing industries. With better healthcare, people are living longer and seek quality-of-life settings in which to reside. Don't call them nursing homes anymore. Now they are Continuous Care Residential Centers (CCRCs), many as high-rise apartment buildings. In buying CCRC condominiums, the residents get healthcare, gourmet food service, and planned activities.

One of the first attempts to crack the growing eldercare market by putting together joint ventures was a group of high-rises financed by my client, a Wall Street investment banking firm. We teamed with branches of the military to build towers in San Antonio, Texas. Air Force Village and the Army Residential Center became beacons for "best years" residential settings for the families of retired military officers. The key selling points were that joint ventures made the projects operational and at no cost to the U.S. taxpayers.

Throughout the years, thematic retirement communities have become profitable investments for major hotel chains, cartels of private investors, and faith-based organizations. Reflecting upon this success, we worked with homebuilders, who spawned upscale housing tract developments in communities of various sizes, inner-city neighborhoods, and redevelopment zones. I gave one the theme for its strategic planning, also reflected in their marketing: "The future has a new address."

Producers of energy often joint venture to create independent drilling or marketing entities. This includes shared offshore platforms and exploration in new regions of the world.

An industry alliance is often needed to create a lobbying arm and public awareness campaign. In the late 1970s, the U.S. Food and Drug Administration banned the food additive known as saccharine, claiming that it contributed to causing cancer. In order to regain the product's standing, its industry leaders teamed with medical professionals, researchers, nonprofit organizations, and citizen groups.

The resulting joint venture was an entity known as the Calorie Control Council. The objective was to call attention to positive uses from saccharine, distance it from other chemical products that were rightfully recalled, and distinguish the need for lowering sugar in diets for health reasons. This national campaign coalesced grassroots support, which caused Congress to overturn the FDA ban on saccharine, which returned the product to market. The result was staggering on the growing diet food market and for those healthcare programs that advocated better dietary controls.

In the early days of television (1950–55), the New York network establishment insisted that all of the shows be performed live. They had a vested interest in keeping production in New York. The Hollywood film community wanted to get involved with the new medium in producing filmed programming. The major studios saw television as a threat and resisted partnerships with the TV networks.

It was the independent production companies that started the joint venture bandwagon rolling. Entrepreneurs such as Desi Arnaz and Dick Powell created the model for independent program production on film. The major Hollywood factories had no choice but to follow suit, but had to modify their old studio system models to conform production for the new medium. The phenomenon of the big guys emulating the practices and achieving the success of the entrepreneurs is what led to the domination of filmed product on television. This progression is indicative of how many business innovations occur and then go mainstream. (For the full story on this, please read my previous book, *The Classic Television Reference.*)

Many companies have found that doing business in a new country is easier when a consortium operates. I learned more about this process while working with a group of Mexican construction, real estate, banking, and factoring companies. They organized an American umbrella corporation in order to sustain a more global presence in the building and marketing of condominiums.

Hardware, software, and component producers are revolutionizing the next generation of technology. AgriSoft was a joint venture of farming cooperatives and software producers. The result was a host of software and processes that maximize efficiencies for farm crop production. Hewlett-Packard spun off Agilent Technologies to become a process systems consulting firm. Agilent installs equipment, systems connectors, and hundreds of pieces of connectivity apparatus from partners as part of its service for industry.

Scientists often joint venture with research institutions, alliances, and licensing entities. Some of the largest included the Superconductor, gene medicine, nano-technology, and homeland security devices.

Contractors and subcontractors often joint venture with large governmental entities such as NASA and military bases. It was through the school district performance review (referenced in Chapter 3) that the opportunities to privatize food catering, bus fleet, and building maintenance services arose, with entrepreneurs creating joint ventures to provide services. The privatization of municipal services such as garbage collection also fits into this category. The construction industry is all about joint venturing, with the general contractors, specialty contractors, and service providers in major building projects.

Group marketing programs are common joint ventures, such as those with auto dealer clusters, municipalities for economic development, tourism destinations, and trade association image upgrades. Co-branding in the hospitality industry has a prominent relationship with cross-selling each other's products. The Partnership for Improved Air Travel served to lobby funds for airport upgrades and call public attention toward travel safety dynamics. The Buy Recycled program partnered with state land offices and environmental groups, promoting cost-effective products that were also environmentally friendly. The Silicon Valley network promoted and created further opportunities for technology companies to flourish.

I worked with Louisiana's tourism industry in its comeback from the Katrina setbacks. It was critical for each community to revisit its own travel and tourism programs. The crisis allowed each venue to rethink strategies, something that ongoing planning customarily inspires. As we learned from the industrial redevelopment of cities in transition (referenced in Chapter 3), wake-up calls to steer course result in creative partnerships to get the job done.

Business units were created for underserved and minority markets by teaming companies of all sizes. I worked with a state government in developing a program to find, train, and get work for women- and minority-owned businesses. It was not enough just to get on bid lists. The agency offered extensive training on best practices, including partnering. By opening doors for solid companies, this stimulated the notion of teamwork in a society that is still full of lone rangers.

Human capital, Branch 4 of the Business Tree, is the most important and still neglected facet of organizations. Under this branch, I still recommend that companies shore up their talent, lest key people defect elsewhere. One of the industries that I have watched evolve throughout the last 30 years is the employee search and staffing industry. They started out performing searches for client companies. Then, they added services to companies needing to downsize or retrain certain executive talent. Administaff and other employee-leasing companies serve turnkey functions, including training. Some companies offer "rent a CEO," "rent a CFO," and other temporary executive engagement situations.

I wish that human services firms would recruit freelance talent. I envision companies and Websites where professional service providers could get engagements, and the companies could get commissions. They could help client companies create best practices, training, performance reviews, and accountability plans as they relate to board members. Another vacant niche where I see great potential is for board members. Had such processes been utilized, many corporate scandals, downturns, and cutbacks could have been avoided.

Research shows that our workforce needs three times the amount of training that it now gets in order to remain competitive. With company layoffs and cutbacks, much of the workforce has been forced to retrain and go after different job niches. One of the growth industries has been education. With much of the workforce needing retraining and professional development, new educational streams have emerged. Traditional universities and colleges now have competition through workforce retraining programs, distance learning, online education, trade schools, and private institutions expanding into each others' backyards. At first, academia resisted, creating gaps where the other providers gained ground. Now, educational institutions have reacted to all this competition by creating joint venture programs and student services, teaming also with community niches.

Other examples of often-practiced joint ventures include international trade development, educators in the creation and revision of curriculum materials, credit unions working with schools to offer thrift plans, distribution centers and networks for retail products, and telecommunications industry service providers. Still more examples of joint ventures include airline partner programs, banks appearing in grocery store spaces, practice management companies with healthcare institutions, and corporate liaisons with fitness facilities as part of employee assistance programs.

Business Tree lesson: Consortium members support each other in developing their own businesses, offering referrals. Those who do it the best will continue to real higher benefits in the future.

The Power of Multiple Partners

Businesses do not exist in a vacuum, nor can they afford to float alone. They must interact with the outside world, predict the trends, and master front-burner issues affecting the climate and opportunities in which they function. In today's global economy where lightning speed is required to get ahead and stay ahead of the competition, no company can be successful without partnering or joint venturing.

Situations that call for teams to collaborate, paralleling branches on the Business Tree, include:

1. **Business Characteristics:** Most industries and core business segments cannot be effectively served by one specialty. It is imperative that multiple disciplines within the core business muster their resources.

2. **Circumstances:** People get thrown together by necessity and sometimes by accident. They are not visualized as a team and often start at cross-purposes. Few participants are taught how to best utilize each participant's respective expertise. Through osmosis, a working relationship evolves.

3. **Economics:** In today's downsized business environment, outsourcing, privatization, and consortiums are fulfilling the work. Larger percentages of contracts are awarded each year to those who exemplify and justify their team approaches. Those who solve business problems and predict future challenges will be retained. Numerically, collaboration contracts are more likely to be renewed.

4. **Demands of the Marketplace:** Savvy business owners know that no one supplier can accomplish it all. Accomplished managers want teams that give value-added service to their organizations, create new ideas, and work effectively. Consortiums must continually improve, in order to justify investments.

5. **Creating New Products:** There are only four ways to grow one's business: sell more products-services, cross-sell existing customers, create new products-services, and joint venture to create new opportunities, which cannot be accomplished without teaming with others.

6. **Opportunities:** Once one makes the commitment to collaborate, circumstances will define the exact teaming structures. The best opportunities are created.

7. **Commitment Toward Partnering:** Those of us who have collaborated with other professionals and organizations know the value. Once one sees the profitability and the power of multiple talents, then one aggressively advocates the teaming processes. It is difficult to work in a vacuum thereafter. Creative partnerships don't just happen. They are pursued.

Collaborations, partnering, and joint venturing are not to be thought of just as shrouds to get business, where subcontractors may later be found to do the work. They are not where one partner presents the work of others as his/her own or where one party misrepresents his/her capabilities, in such a way as to overshadow the promised team approach. They are also NOT:

- Where one partner treats others more like subcontractors or vendors.
- Where one participant keeps other collaborators away from the client's view.
- Ego fiefdoms, where one participant assumes a demeanor that harms the project.
- Where cost considerations preclude all partners from being utilized.
- Where one partner steals business from another.
- Where non-partners are given advantageous position over ground-floor members who paid their dues in securing the work.

- Where one or more parties is knowingly used for their knowledge and then dismissed.

The kinds of companies that do not want to collaborate include those that have never had to collaborate, partner, or joint venture before. There are some that don't believe in the concept and usually give nebulous reasons why. It includes those that want only to be the center of attention and those that fear being compared to others of stature in their own right. Some are afraid that their process or expertise will not stand the test when compared with others. Finally, there are those that had one or two bad experiences with partnering in the past, usually because they were on the periphery or really weren't equal partners in the first place.

Characteristics of Good Collaborators

The kinds of companies that want to collaborate include those that are good and are willing to do what it takes to get progressively better. My experience is that those who have captained their own teams make better partners, knowing the value of being a good member of someone else's team.

The best collaborators include those who do their best work in collaboration with others and those who appreciate creativity and new challenges. Leaders who have been mentored already have a sense of self-worth and have a bona fide track record on their own. Their companies have a commitment toward knowledge enhancement, walk the talk by their interactions with others, and appreciate fresh ideas, especially from unexpected sources.

Veteran partners have been on other teams in the past, with case studies of actual collaborations. They have successes and failures to their credit, with an understanding of the causal factors, outcomes, and lessons learned.

Steps Toward Collaboration Success

There are seven levels of building successful liaisons. These apply to working with business partners, as well as building customer relationships:

1. **Want to Get Business:** Players are seeking a rub-off effect, success by association. Partnering sounds good to the marketplace. Nothing ventured, nothing gained. Why not give the premise a try?

2. **Want to Garner Ideas:** Companies then want to learn more about the customers. Each team member must commit to professional development, taking the program to a higher level. Making sales calls (mandated or voluntarily) does not constitute relationship-building.

3. **First Attempts:** Team members conduct programs that get early results, praise, and requests for more. At this point, they realize that playing well with others is not so bad and that there is an art to doing so effectively.

4. **Mistakes, Successes, and Lessons Learned:** Competition, marketplace changes, or urgent need led the initiative to begin. Customer retention and enhancement programs require that a cohesive team approach with multiple talents be continued.

5. **Continued Collaborations:** Collaborators truly understand teamwork and have had prior successful experiences at customer service. The sophisticated ones are skilled at building and utilizing colleagues and outside experts.

6. **Advocate Teamwork:** Consortium members want to learn from each other. All share the project

risks equally. Early successes have inspired deeper activity. Business relationship-building is considered an ongoing process, not a "once in a while" action or marketing gimmick.

7. **Team Up Quite Often:** There exists an ongoing commitment in these sophisticated companies toward the concept and each other. Each team member realizes something of value from the partnership and continues to give back. Customers recommend and freely refer business to the consortium. What benefits one partner will indeed benefit all.

The biggest successes with collaborations came when a crisis or urgent need forced the client to hire a consortium. Time deadlines and nature of the project required a cohesive team approach. The work required multiple professional skills. Consortium members were tops in their fields.

Successful consortium members truly understood teamwork and had prior successful experiences in joint venturing. Consortium members wanted to learn from each other. Early successes spurred future collaborations. Joint venturing was considered an ongoing process, not just a "once in a while" action. Each team member realized something of value. The client recommended the consortium to others, which enabled it to continue and get more effective.

My own disappointments with previous collaborations occurred because of a failure of participants to understand and thus utilize each others' talents. One or more participants had a past unfortunate experience and tended to over-generalize about the worth of consortiums. It was toxic when one partner put another down on the basis of academic credentials or some professional designation that sets himself/herself apart from other team members.

In consortiums that fail, the participants exhibit the "lone-ranger syndrome," preferring the comfort of trusting the one person they have counted upon. Partnerships fail when participants exhibit the "I can do that" syndrome, thinking that they do the same exact things that other consortium members do and, thus, see no value in working together, sharing projects, and referring business.

Junior associates of consortiums wreak havoc when they want to hoard the billing dollars in-house, to look good to their superiors, enhance their billable quotas, or fulfill other objectives that they are not sophisticated enough to identify. Toxic to teamwork is when junior associates of consortium members refuse to recognize the seniority and wisdom of other associates, utilizing the power of the budget to control creative thoughts and strategic thinking of subcontractors.

There are excellent reasons to give the concept of teamwork a chance. Think of the projects that got away—the business opportunities that a team could have created. Think of contracts that were awarded to others who exhibited much more of a team approach. Learn from industries where consortiums are the rule, rather than the exception, such as aerospace, energy, construction, research, and high-tech.

The marketplace is continually changing. Subcontractor, supplier, support talent, and vendor information can be shared. Consortiums are inevitable. If we don't do it early, others will beat us to it.

Benefits for participating principals and firms include an ongoing association and professional exchange with the best in respective fields. Utilize professional synergy to create opportunities that individuals could not. Serve as a beacon for professionalism. Provide access to experts otherwise not known to potential clients. Refer and cross-sell each others' services. Through demands uncovered, develop programs and materials to meet markets.

Take a Look. Improve. Everyone Benefits.

This final section of the chapter centers upon an area that encompasses both leadership and teamwork skills. This is an area of business where few top executives were ever mentored.

This section is a primer on awards programs, recognition, the attention they bring, and the ultimate benefits of continuous improvement, plus the inspiration to keep doing an excellent job.

Awards and recognition are very important for businesses. Everyone likes to be associated with a winner. If certain kinds of companies have not received awards, one might rightfully suspect why. Such is the status of modern society.

There are some companies whose quest for recognition goes to extremes. However, those who do good work should indeed be recognized publicly for it. Tooting one's horn is a reflection of excellent work, and one need not be embarrassed by external recognition. Awards become a marketing tool and, more importantly, become the call to keep besting one's company in the eyes of customers, employees, and stakeholders.

I have won more than 150 awards in my long career. Most were for client projects in juried competitions. Many were for civic leadership and service to non-profit causes. A few were awarded by virtue of staying power in a variety of business and community arenas. In addition to that were the certificates, children's artwork, photos, and other memorabilia presented as thanks for acts of kindness, garnered from decades of doing things that I just saw as being a good citizen.

In some cultures, the notion of achieving notoriety, winning awards, championing civic causes, and attaining notoriety for your company is unheard of. A few years ago, I was asked by the Japanese-American Chamber of Commerce to write a handbook on giving back to the community and why it is important in the Western world. This is contrary to the low-profile stance that business leaders take in Asia, Latin America, and the Middle East.

While speaking and consulting businesses in Kuwait, I was asked to present a program on the Western world's non-profit culture and why business must get involved with causes. Often in work in Latin America and Europe, questions about the value of cause-related marketing came up from interested parties wishing to participate but wondering how far to go in attracting attention to themselves.

When you win enough awards in your career, one gets asked to judge other programs. In my case, those included programs for the Malcolm Baldridge Quality Award, United Way of America, National Association for Community Leadership, Associated General Contractors, American Education Association, Harvard Business School, and others. Each time, I was honored to volunteer time and serve. Each time, I learned much and was inspired by those honorable, sincere companies who applied. As a judge, you want everyone to do well, and you believe all of them to be winners.

Through my membership in a think tank called the Silver Fox Advisors, I joined my friends in judging as Better Business Bureau awards program. As one who works with the world's largest corporations, I was there reading application forms from movers, janitorial service companies, mechanics, plumbers, technology providers, and the entire rainbow of local small business.

You could tell that company owners were stretching beyond their comfort zones to answer all the questions. These were low-key people who just worked hard and served their customers well. Now, the entrants had to write their business philosophies for outsiders to review. Though these narratives may not reflect the weighty language that I use in this book, they indeed reflected a group of sincere company owners who were trying to do their very best. Their answers to questions about ethical dilemmas and putting customer crises first were the kinds of comments that bureaucracy-ridden corporations would never be caught rendering. I wondered why all businesses cannot be as honorable and responsive as those small business owners who entered that program.

Subsequently, fellow awards judge Butch Madrazo and I appeared on a radio show to promote the awards winners. The CEO of one of the winning companies said that the application made him think long and hard about his business, being totally honest about many facets and uncovering needs for improvement in other areas. Bravo for his insights. I stated that awards applications should be thought of as executive summaries for company strategic plans. These analyses should then become the lynchpin for the next visioning process and how the organization will vault top the next tier.

One year, I had received several awards. I got a Savvy Award, for the top three community leaders. I was a Dewar's profile subject. I had gotten a standing ovation at the United Nations for volunteer work that was my honor to do (especially because it enabled me to work with my favorite actress, Audrey Hepburn).

Subsequently, I was participating in a community stewardship awards judging. I quizzed, "Why is it that the same old names keep popping up? There are great people to honor other that those of us from business, high society, or other top-of-the-mind awareness. What this community needs is an awards program that people like us cannot win."

I was then challenged to come up with such a program, the result being the Leadership in Action Awards for the city of Houston. I wrote a four-page application that was long and detailed, asking some very tough questions. To enter this program, non-profit organizations in each category (arts, education, health causes, diversity, and so forth) had to enter as teams, not as individuals. They had to justify donations, volunteer usage, partnerships, in-kind services, public sector support, and other criteria. Then they had to answer accountability and program evaluation questions.

We staged a seminar for prospective entrants and gave pointers on filling out the complete application, to help avoid the boilerplate material that some might otherwise submit. Those who attended the application preparation seminar did indeed fare better in the judging process. At the judging, we were all impressed with how well these "unsung heroes" in the community described their non-profit programs.

At the awards presentation banquet, the swell of pride from the winning organizations, their directors, their volunteers, and even some of their clients was heartening to see. These unsung heroes were finally getting their just recognition for community work well done. The corporate donors who supported them had every right to be proud.

At the following year's awards preparation seminar, the previous year's winners also spoke. One said that it was the toughest application they had ever filled out. They had since submitted material contained in our application to foundations and gotten more funding than expected because they volunteered so much more information than had been required. Because their awards were based upon genuine team efforts, these programs received much more support from their boards, funding sources, and constituencies.

I believe that every business must go after some forms of recognition because the process offers levels of objective judgment and criticism necessary to sustain the business. One cannot go after awards just for glorification reasons. However, recognition programs are a balanced scorecard that involves the scrutiny of the company and its leaders by credible outside sources.

Awards inspire companies of all sizes to work harder and try more creative things. Good deeds in the community are not done for the awards; they just represent good business. Receiving recognition after the fact for works that were attempted for right and noble reasons is the icing on the cake that employees need. Good people aspire to higher goals. Every business leader needs to be groomed as a community leader.

Business Tree lesson: Recognition for a track record of contributions represents more than "tooting one's own horn." It is indicative of the kind of organizations with which you are honored to do business. The more that one is recognized and honored, the harder that one works to keep the luster and its integrity shiny.

• ● •

Every community should sponsor a business awards recognition program. If the municipality does not have one, it should start such a program. Potential co-sponsors could include newspapers, Better Business Bureau chapters, business schools, chambers of commerce, Rotary and other service clubs, professional associations, and non-profit community leadership organizations.

The process of entering juried awards competition should be seen as the next step toward company visioning. The narrative becomes an executive summary for the next strategic plan. Awards for which someone else nominates you are meritorious honors, reflecting your body of work and well-earned reputation.

Being the recipient of awards gives you the opportunity to market your company in a tasteful manner. Always reframe the recognition back to the customers, as a recommitment toward serving them better and further.

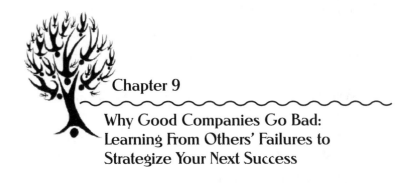

Chapter 9

Why Good Companies Go Bad: Learning From Others' Failures to Strategize Your Next Success

If you keep doing what you're doing, then you'll keep getting what you've gotten in the past. Most organizations rely upon what I call *weapons of mass distraction,* a series of excuses, platitudes, illogical assumptions, and reasons why they will not look forward and cannot move forward.

This chapter studies the barriers that prevent companies from moving ahead, such as obsolete or out-of-touch management styles and corporate cultures, emphasis on the wrong business niches, improper advice from consultants, and the downstream results of resisting change. We can learn how to surmount them and build structures that will avoid them in the future.

Business organizations are like trees: They seemingly look the same from day to day. To the untrained eye, most resemble each other. After all, they are just trees!

There are many types of businesses in today's global economy. Many factors affect their ability to grow, much less their chances for longevity. Many types of trees exist in the environment:

- Seeds just planted (startup companies).

- Young, fledgling trees (companies with promise).

- Skinny, underfed trees (companies operating lean and mean, yet needing to be nourished).

- Overfed trees (companies with too much debt and layers of bureaucracy).

- Malnourished trees, dropping leaves, limbs, bark, and other shapes of life.

- Trees diagnosed as "near death," where major surgery is needed in order to keep them alive (companies that are ripe for takeover).

- Dying trees, which are dark shadows of their former selves (companies in reorganization bankruptcy).

- Virtually dead trees, awaiting the final death pronouncement.

- Formerly diagnosed trees that rebound at the last minute to live.

- Near-death trees that claim to have rebounded but that should have already been put out of their misery.

- Buds from fallen trees that are now sprouting organizations on their own.

- Surgically transplanted tree sections that are now taking on their own lives (divisions that were spun off as new companies).

- Droppings from old trees that are not doing any better in their new environment. They brought most of the bad sap from their former tree with them.

Some trees (organizations) can only grow in certain environments. Palm trees only thrive in arid climates and near bayou seepage. Pine trees are found only in heavily wooded areas. Some trees are intended for limited usage, such as Christmas trees.

The same holds true for their other cousins of trees, including potted plants, floral arrangements, seasonal gardening plants, bushes, hedges, shrubs, moss, vines, and decorative landscaping. These are analogous to the various kinds of small service companies that feed into the larger companies, with the environment being analogous to a robust business continuum.

Different Trees in the Forest

Management makes fatal mistakes in assuming that trees (businesses) are guaranteed by nature to grow (be productive and profitable), without doing anything more than just stand there (doing business as usual). Many believe that comparable-sized trees (businesses) have equivalent life, purpose, and shareholder value.

Other misperceptions about status quo businesses made by people include:

- Trees (businesses) have more similarities than differences and, thus, can be run about the same.

- Trees (businesses) live pretty much on their own, without nurturing (maintenance) or relationship to others in the landscape.

- Keepers of the property can do as they please, without respect to the environment (customer base, marketplace).

- Branches (business components) keep pretty much to themselves, rather than relating to the tree (organization) as a whole.

- Limbs (divisions, sections, units) relate to their own branch and engage in heavy turf protection.

- Twigs (professional resources) are expected to fall and are easily replaceable.

- Leaves (facilities, equipment, technologies) are expected to fall and are easily replaceable.

- Parts of the tree should fend for themselves (be self-contained profit centers) without relating to the whole tree (seamless concept of a company).

- Nobody knows how the trunk or roots get there. It's just expected that they remain.

- Once trees (businesses) have been serviced, then no further maintenance actions are required.

Why Companies Get Lost, Starve, Wither, and Die

Addictive Organizations miss their opportunities by making scapegoats of people who are the messengers of change. They fight change in every shape, form, or concept. Management of these companies are unable to listen and refuse to hear that change is coming and what worked in the past is no longer effective. Their failure to reinvent and fear of new strategies results in a comfort level that promotes institutional mediocrity, false pride, and risk avoidance.

Down-Cycle Companies, stuck in a downward trending economic morass, show a preoccupation with deals, rather than with the hard work of running and improving an ongoing operation. Their inaccessibility to independent thinkers results in a failure to benchmark results and learn from accomplishments.

Head-in-the-Sand Companies find that there are high costs associated with their lack of will and foresight, including the expenses of cleaning up problems, waste, poor controls, and lack of employee motivation and activity. High costs are incurred and management's energy is wasted on reworking shoddy product, making good on inferior work, patching up quality controls, and dealing with employee problems. They continue band-aid surgeries, creating six-fold operational costs per year and more barriers to progress.

Coming From Behind Companies constantly struggle due to poor locations, under-capitalization, unsuccessful marketing, and unprofitable pricing. These include chain stores and franchises—good ideas that failed in their applications.

Passive Companies don't bother to strategize toward the future and are continually wounded by events. They react to events instead of anticipating them. They engage in recovery and restoration, and catch-up activities, and are the victims of bad advice from the wrong consultants. They often suffer from a damaged reputation and don't bother trying to fix it. Their inertia results in no progress, no planning, and outrageous opportunity costs.

Autopilot Companies relive past successes and forget that the future is a moving target and an ever-changing marketplace. They are tradition bound, sticking to what worked in the past, even unto bankruptcy. They can't get beyond past accomplishments, and "tradition" becomes a rationale for refusing to change.

None of these companies recognize that events will overtake them, and that formulas for past successes can practically guarantee future failures. To get to the next tier—or merely to sustain a measure of success—they must continually look toward the future. To that end, strategic planning and corporate visioning are essential. Using the tools provided in the book, businesses can appraise where they are going next and how to refocus as long-lasting companies.

These are the many reasons why good organizations of all sizes go astray, categorized per each branch of the Business Tree.

Branch 1: The Business You're In

The company was founded because of a core in which the founders had expertise. Methods and technologies were probably developed from past companies. In this new enterprise, the founders brought over the experiences and corporate cultures. Core industry managers-personnel-consultants focus only on their own niche, without a holistic relationship to the rest of the tree-organization.

The service is rendered, and products are designed and manufactured the same way in which they always were. Technical abilities and specialties are not further developed after the company's initial successes in creating their widget. The presumption held is that, if it worked for the company founders, then it still works for the rest of the industry and all competitors within it.

Management doesn't see the need to use industry consultants or technical specialists. Core business supplier relationships have not been examined or updated lately. No investment has been made toward quality controls.

Branch 2: Running the Business

Core industry people think like their industry training background, not like managers. Professional managers are not given full rein to do their jobs. Administrative, production, and support personnel focus only on their own niche, without holistic relationships to the rest of the tree-organization.

The company continues to be run as it has always operated, citing the first way of doing things as a "tradition." Top management subscribes to the philosophy of "if it ain't broke, don't fix it."

A lack of formal organizational structure leaves many company executives blamable but not accountable, with many unclear as to their roles and responsibilities. Practices, procedures, operations, and structure are not documented in writing, nor are they communicated to employees. Measuring performance is not factored into the production continuum. Management asks, "Why bother to review everything? Let's just do it."

The physical plant is not regularly studied, updated, or modified. Management contends, "It was good enough when we built it and still fits our needs." Cost containment is the main driver of all process applications, technologies, equipment, supplies, and systems. Distribution standards are not documented, practiced, or measured. Time management is not observed, studied, or utilized. The attitude is perpetuated that "when it's ready, it's ready." The company continues to stockpile inventories. No efforts are made to reduce surplus or adopt practices such as just-in-time delivery.

Management does not consult the lawyers until the company gets into trouble or is sued. The organization rarely outsources. The prevailing attitude is: "We have enough engineers and technicians working for us. Why pay others on the outside?"

The administrative function does not have a written, formal purchasing plan. "When we need something, just send out for it." To cut expenses, repair and maintenance contracts are not held and are often not renewed. Equipment is bought outright, rather than leased or financed.

Continuous quality improvement is not practiced. No consideration is given toward creating or implementing such a program. The company applies band-aid surgery toward process and operations facets—but only at such time they absolutely have to or are forced to.

Branch 3: Financial

Profit is the driver, without all the techniques necessary to optimize. In other companies, the opposite is true, continuing to do what they've been doing, without adequate financial controls and accountabilities. Many companies function at one extreme or the other: bean-counter mentality or slipshod approach to business.

The belief is held that every product must make a profit, at all times. Few, if any, profits are plowed back into the business. Few long-term investments are made. The company's book of assets is not adequately valued or managed. Owners believe that the only reason for being in business is to make as much money for themselves as possible.

Cash flow, forecasting, and budgeting are inconsistent, if they're monitored at all. Policies with receivables are not formal, and squeaky wheels get the grease. The business officer does not concern himself about equity and debt financing. The contention is that such things are only applicable to public companies.

The company does not consult the accounting firm until tax season or audit time. Banking and investing relationships are not fully valued. Creditor payments are made as late as possible, even paying past-due interest. The game is to keep creditors waiting, using their money interest-free, without realizing the costs of administrative minutia. The company has gotten a reputation for being slow-pay. The accounts-payable officer never mediates differences with creditors until they sue, figuring that, if one wears creditors down, they will hopefully go away.

Finance charges are paid at maximum rates. No attempt has been made to negotiate volume discounts. The company buys the cheapest insurance, which leaves company employees under-covered, unnecessarily bothered by third-party red tape, and not as focused on company loyalty as they could be.

Financial managers-personnel-consultants focus only on their own niche, without a holistic relationship with the rest of the tree-organization.

Branch 4: People

Employees are not empowered. Job descriptions, evaluations, and advancements are nebulous. Management has limited people skills. Training is nominal and inconsistent.

The corporate culture is slow paced, sluggish, and without professionalism. Employees are complacent and rarely carry the company banner forward. Low morale persists and builds upon itself. The human resources department hires only to fill vacant jobs rather than to match talent to potential company opportunities.

Top management does not see itself as needing to have people-development, skills, or team-building responsibilities. Only executives get bonuses. Others should be grateful to get a regular paycheck. The boss takes the attitude that "Those people work for me. I don't work for them." A regular paycheck is thought to be the only and best incentive for people to work.

Upon hiring, employees are handed nebulous job descriptions and are supposed to perform. If they don't, they're fired. Management believes that troublesome employees are easily replaceable and does not realize the economic sense of saving productive workers. Executives see themselves as being the heart of this company. They do the real work, especially the ones the CEO brought on board.

The value of training is not understood, appreciated, or related to employee performance or the bottom line. They ask, "Why spend money on professional development?" The company develops and teaches all workshops and seminars with in-house talent. The value of outsourced training by niche experts is not comprehended.

Management does not know how to discern among or properly utilize business consultants. To cover its lack of analytical ability, it queries, "Why do consultants keep looking at how the organization operates? They cannot possibly know what we know."

Performance reviews are arbitrary and are never held with any regularity, nor are employees judged against viable corporate objectives. Empowerment, team-building, and people-skills programs are seen as necessary evils and are minimized.

Branch 5: Business Development

The company does not do the things necessary to capture or maintain market share. Sales are static or drop. The company does not sell enough to pay its overhead, forcing cutbacks, downsizing, and dropping product lines. Promotional activities are for ego purposes, rather than focusing upon key business needs, opportunities, and issues.

The company does not have a clearly defined image or communications strategy. Branding depends upon the boss's latest whim or whatever company he wants to copy. The communications section manager is never in the planning or production loops, nor is he/she asked to advise corporate management.

No formal, written, or measurable sales plan exists. Goals are either unreasonably high or dangerously low. Marketing and sales are viewed as the same concepts. No formal marketing plan exists. Marketing is done on a whim or after the fact. The sales force is not valued and is seen as a necessary evil. Sales and marketing people are under-trained, under-managed, and threatened with termination for not meeting quotas, with an axe poised over their heads.

No formal written advertising program exists. No formal written public relations program exists. Advertising and public relations are viewed as the same thing and, thus, are lumped together in management's consciousness. Incentives, advertising specialties, and customer appreciation are not factored into the marketing budget. Creative work is done in-house. Thus, expenses are incurred to fully staff a creative services department.

Top management does not see itself as needing to maintain or contribute to business development responsibilities. Incorrect assumptions preclude an aggressive communications strategy. Management says, "The marketplace knows who we are. Why should we have to adapt?" Marketing and sales are viewed only as necessary evils. Engineers and other core business practitioners disdain the concepts and do not fully cooperate with marketing and sales.

Sales and marketing personnel focus only on their own niche, without a holistic relationship to the rest of the tree-organization.

Category 6: Body of Knowledge

The company doesn't fully understand the relationship of each of the branches to the others. Management doesn't know or care what's going on outside their doors. Research is not conducted. The trunk is limp and weak, keeping roots from living well.

Because managers-personnel-consultants focused only on their own niches, no holistic relationship to the rest of the tree-organization was ever developed. Each niche protects its own turf.

The company maintains a false sense of success, rarely attributing the contributions of employees and blaming others for management's own shortcomings. The company remains stuck in a complacent mode, with an inability to predict or stay ahead of trends. Decision-makers never learn the lessons of failure or the true reasons for successes. The company follows its industry, rather than leading. Product and service development take place after its competitors do the innovating.

Management keeps its head in the sand. The rationale is that "nothing that goes on outside our company affects our business in any way." There is an unwillingness to invest in research or to comprehend how it might impact corporate growth. There is a reluctance to joint venture or work with other companies. Some contend, "They just want to steal our customers."

It is believed that government agencies and regulators are to be avoided, feared, fought, or ignored. It is wrongly believed that a free market does not need regulations at all, which is not true. Company leadership feels that it does not owe anything back to the communities in which it works, nor does it have the need to interface with them.

Category 7: The Big Picture

Change was never comprehended or mastered. Applying band-aid surgery to problems keeps the company from ever having to create, face, or benchmark against a big picture. No shared vision is ever crafted, let alone articulated and followed. Low corporate self-esteem persists.

The organization does not sprout healthy roots. Existing roots wither away, many dying before their time. The biggest perpetrators of the problems move on to "greener pastures," taking the same malnourishments with them.

Strategic planning is viewed as a superfluous exercise that is only applicable to companies other than ours. Strategic planning is done when the boss goes away for the weekend and comes back with a list of things to be executed by others. The assumption is that a common corporate culture is held by the entire organization.

Bad companies have so many other rationales to offer:

"Whatever the company thinks, so will all of its employees."

"Outside-the-box thinking does not apply to us, nor will be tolerated. What is it, anyway?"

"We do not engage in unethical practices. What is an ethics statement?"

"The quality process means doing things the way we've always done them, without deviation or interference by unwanted intruders."

At best, change will be tolerated in bad companies. Most resources have already been expended to fight and prevent change from occurring. No crisis management, preparedness, or prevention program exists. Management deals with each crisis as it comes up. The CEO remains isolated from creative, contrary, or differing viewpoints. Corporate purges result from isolationism. Creative business practices are not welcome, sought, or achieved.

Categories of Business
High Costs

1. Cleaning up problems. Waste, spoilage. Poor controls. Downtime. Lack of employee motivation and activity.

2. Rework. Product recalls. Make good for shoddy or inferior work. Poor location. Red tape. Excess overhead.

3. Missed marks. Poor controls on quality. Fallout damage from employees with problems. Undercapitalization. Unsuccessful marketing. Unprofitable pricing.

4. Damage control. Crisis management. Lawsuits because procedures were not upheld. Violations of codes. Disasters due to employee carelessness, oversights, etc. Factors outside your company that impede your ability to do business.

5. Recovery and restoration. Repairing wrong actions. Empty activities. Cleanups, corrections, and adaptations. Employee turnover, rehiring, and retraining. Bad advice from the wrong consultants. Repairing a damaged company reputation.

6. Retooling, restarting. Wrong use of company resources. Converting codes-standards. Chasing wrong leads, prospects, or markets. Damage caused by inertia, lack of progress. "Business as usual" philosophy. Expenses incurred by taking quick fixes.

7. Opportunity costs. Failure to understand what business they're really in. Inability to read warning signs or understand external influences. Failure to change. Inability to plan. Over-dependence on one product or service line. Diversifying beyond the scope of company expertise. Lack of an articulated, well-implemented vision.

Contributing Factors of High Business Costs

1. Failure to value and optimize true company resources.

2. Poor premises, policies, processes, procedures, precedents, and planning.

3. Opportunities not heeded or capitalized.

4. The wrong people, in the wrong jobs. Under-trained employees.

5. The wrong consultants (miscast, untrained, improperly used).

6. Lack of articulated focus and vision. With no plan, no journey will be completed.

7. Lack of movement really means falling behind the pack and eventually losing ground.

What Could Have Reduced the High Costs

1. Effective policies and procedures.

2. Setting and respecting boundaries.

3. Realistic expectations and measurements.

4. Training and development of human capital/people.

5. Commitments to quality.

6. Strategic planning.

7. Organizational vision.

Stages of Addressing Business Strategy Dilemmas

This seven-stage process has proven to be the progression of addressing such dilemmas in organizations:

1. Apply band-aid surgery for what management thinks is the problem. One problem looks solved. Look the other way, or else its stitches will come undone. The result is a band-aid surgery mindset that perpetuates itself.

2. Fix what vendors who are selling their "consultative services" tell the company needs to be fixed. The company becomes holding to a patchwork of vendors, not a cohesive diagnosis of the organization's needs. Shoot the messenger when you don't get the answers that you want or expect.

3. Fix what will make management look like problem-solvers. Conduct look-good activities, which unravel as band-aid surgeries soon enough. Steer clear of recommendations that will facilitate change in the organization.

4. Perform patchwork to cover bases and rear-ends. Pursue reactive projects, rather than business strategies. The rationale is that the rear end that is exposed will embarrass the whole organization.

5. Earnest initial efforts to solve actual problems with effective procedures always will draw earnest initial results. But don't rest upon early laurels. Embody sincere intents to try harder and activities that are proactive in nature.

6. Management learns and holds deep insights as to the real problems and causes. It takes courage to focus clearly, then to take decisive actions. Enlightened leadership relishes the journey. Paradigm shifts, empowered employees, and heightened productivity result.

7. At this level, planning, strategies and measurements for the long-term are the norm. In a planned growth organization, each challenge is met successfully.

Levels of Handling Problems, as Reflected in Business Strategy

Research shows that 92 percent of all problems in organizations stem from poor management decisions. There are progressive levels that companies in trouble tend to handle problems. They include:

1. **Do Nothing:** Uninformed management thinks that things will work themselves out or that the causes of problems will go away. Research shows that doing nothing results in creating at least six more affiliated problems.

2. **Deny or Avoid:** Management doesn't see problems as such, keeping their heads in the sand and remaining impervious to warning signs of trouble. They go to great lengths to put positive spins on anything that may point back to one's self, department, or organization as being problematic.

3. **Gloss Over the Problems:** Cover-ups cost six to 12 times that of addressing problems upfront. In addition to financial, corporate scandal cover-up costs can include the effects upon morale, activity levels, productivity, decision-making, creativity, adaptation, and innovation. Even after the cover-up has fully played out, there is an additional cost: the period of recovery and restoration of confidence.

4. **Partially Address:** When management performs band-aid surgery, at such time as action is demanded, it addresses the signs and symptoms, without addressing root causes. This shows that something is being done, but it is often the wrong thing at the wrong time.

5. **Handle in Politically Correct Terms:** Some problems are addressed, partially or fully, because bosses, regulators, or stakeholders expect it. Some are handled for fear of repercussion. This motive results in tentative actions, with lip service paid to deep solutions.

6. **Address Head-On:** Problems are, of course, opportunities to take action. Everyone makes mistakes, and success lies in the way that problems are recognized, solved, and learned from. The mark of a true manager is to recognize problems sooner, rather than later. The mark of an effective leader is the ability and willingness to take swift and definitive actions. The mark of an empowered team is its participation in this process. The mark of a successful organization is its endorsement and insistence upon this method of action.

7. **Address in Advance, Preparing for Situations:** Proactively study for patterns. Eighty-five percent of the time, crises that are predicted and pre-addressed are averted. The skill in pre-managing problems is a fundamental tenet of a quality-oriented organization.

Failure to take pro-active business strategies and steps becomes a habit in any organization. Let one thing slide, and another layer of problems will appear. It's easier and more comfortable to look the other way.

Organizations try to maintain the status quo, thinking it to be their best course, by finding greater comfort with the "same old, same old," rather than new concepts. Habits become labeled as "traditions" by the organizations denying the implications of change, hoping their problems will go away and focusing anywhere besides their own culpability with problems. Problems are seemingly swept under the carpet by blaming mistakes away, refusal to take personal accountability, and failure to emphasize the positives.

There are costs attached to neglect, indecision, and non-actions. Failure to take proactive measures costs the organization exponentially each year by six.

You and your company will pay the bills for damage caused by inertia or lack of progress. Waste, spoilage, downtime, and empty activities currently existing bring down productivity and profitability potential.

Lack of having a cohesive marketplace strategy means you're chasing too many of the wrong leads, prospects, or markets, which sets the company back. By sticking to "business as usual," even when it is clearly not what it used to be, companies began telling themselves the great lies that justify their refusal to change and believe them to be truisms.

Long-term expenses incurred by adopting quick fixes and applying band-aid surgery to problems usually result in opening new ones. Possessing an inability to spot where the current and upcoming opportunities result in the company abdicating its marketplace to others. The company falls behind the competition, because of its failure to change, grow, and succeed, plus failure to recognize and reward the strengths within your own organization.

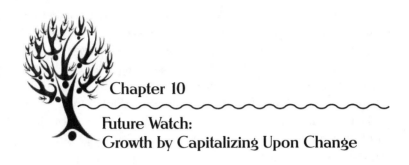

Chapter 10

Future Watch:
Growth by Capitalizing Upon Change

This chapter supports the benefits of changing and moving forward as a result. Companies must detect problems, create opportunities, and assure that planned growth takes place. Those who do so will master change, rather than falling victim to it.

Businesses cannot exist in a vacuum. They must interact with the outside world. They must predict the trends and master the issues affecting the climate and opportunities in which they function. This includes stimulating "outside-the-box" thinking, building customer coalitions, and distinguishing your company from the pack.

The future is a series of journeys along a twisting and turning course, affected by what we choose to do and the priorities that we assign. Along the way, there are warning signs that we either recognize or pay the price later for overlooking. Company futures are determined by choices that we make.

Our present tense and, thus, our future is further influenced by time and resources we spend interacting with other people and the actions of other people, directly or indirectly affecting us. The perspective of future actions is based upon mistakes we make and what we learn from them.

There are several schools of thought on the subject of futurism, depending upon the niche focus of those consultants who embrace the process. Some are marketing-focused and say that the marketplace decides and drives all changes. I say that the marketplace cannot guide itself, and needs to be steered and educated in order to make reasonable demands and foster achievable results. It is important that we not classify futurism as a champion or a subset of marketing, technology, training, or research.

This chapter is intended to take futurism out of the esoteric and into the practice of business. I offer nine of my own definitions for the process of capturing and building a shared vision for organizations to chart their next 10-plus years. Each one gets progressively more sophisticated.

Futurism is what you will do and become, rather than what it is to be. It is what you can and are committed to accomplishing, rather than what mysteriously lies ahead.

Futurism means leaders and organizations taking personal responsibility and accountability for what happens. Abdicating to someone or something else does not constitute business strategy and, in fact, sets the organization backward.

Futurism learns from and benefits from the past, a powerful teaching tool that I call "yesterday-ism." Giving new definitions to old ideas and new meanings to familiar premises, we should learn from the previous successes of others. We must study the business crises and learn from the failures of others. Business must understand the definitive events, cycles, trends, and subtle nuances because they will recur with great regularity.

Futurism means seeing clearly your perspectives and those of others. Growth companies capitalize upon change, rather than becoming a by-product of it. Understand what change is and what it can do for your organization.

Futurism becomes an ongoing quest toward wisdom. The organization commits to learning, which creates knowledge, inspires insights, and culminates in wisdom. It is more than having data that is not interpreted or applied. It is more than just being taught or informed.

Futurism is a mix of ideas that inspire, manage, and benchmark change. The ingredients may change management, crisis management and preparedness, streamlining operations, empowerment of people, re-engineering, quality improvement, marketplace development, organizational evolution, and vision.

Futurism means developing critical thinking and reasoning skills, rather than dwelling just upon techniques and processes. Sales, technology, re-engineering, marketing, research, training, operations, and administration are pieces of a much larger mosaic and should be seen as such. Futurism embodies thought processes that create and energize the mosaic and its pieces.

Futurism results from watching other people changing and capitalizing upon it. Understand from where we came in order to posture where we are headed. Creating organizational vision, setting the stage for all activities, processes, accomplishments, and goals. Efforts must be realistic, and all must be held accountable.

Futurism indeed becomes the foresight to develop hindsight that creates insight into the future.

Change Management

Research shows that change is 90-percent beneficial. So why do people fight what's in their best interest? It occurs because of fears, contexts, decisions, and a tendency to second-guess. Change management is an elixir, not a death sentence.

People and organizations change at the rate of 71 percent per year, without always seeing it occur. The secret with planning-based futurism is to benefit from inevitable changes, rather than become victims of an environment that was changed by others. Although others in the marketplace do not manage change, the successful company reads those signs and creates opportunities to surpass the others.

Companies driven only by money (making it and keeping it) see business as a game, not a philosophy of productivity. Human beings and the organizations that they inhabit are products of change. The manner in which they accept change has a direct relationship to their future success. The ability to adapt, learn, and innovate is the basis of change management. Thriving upon change and mastering it are the fundamentals of futurism.

Developing sophisticated thinking, reasoning, idea-generation, and planning skills is the only way in which organizations and their leaders will survive in the future. Today's workforce will need three times the amount of executive development and leadership training that it now gets—if the organization intends to stay in business, remain competitive, and tackle the future successfully.

Organizations of all sizes must have planning in order to delineate future operations, opportunities, future directions that the company might take, and nuggets of wisdom to help get them to new plateaus.

There is a difference between how one is basically educated and the ingredients needed to succeed in the long term. Many people never amass those ingredients because they stop learning or don't see the need to go any further. Many people think they are "going further" but otherwise spin their wheels.

There is a large disconnect between indoctrinating people to tools of the trade and the myriad elements they will need to assimilate for their own futures. Neither teachers nor students have all the necessary ingredients. It is up to both to obtain skills, inspiration, mentoring, processes, accountability, creativity, and other components from niche experts.

Companies owe it to themselves to think and plan before launching piecemeal training programs. After carefully articulating and understanding direction, then niche project work within the organization will stand a chance of being successful.

Styles and Approaches to Mastering Change		
Low-Power	**Entrepreneur**	**Innovator**
Maintain the status quo.	Carve new opportunities.	Create future paths for others.
Technical proficiency skills.	Develop to an art.	Create new modules.
Caution. Don't rock the boat. Low-profile.	Take bold steps to lead and create new things.	Holds the courage of convictions.
Dependency.	Autonomy.	Self-reliant.
Survival.	Risk and expansion.	Vision, philosophy, future of the business.
Bureaucracy.	Customer orientation.	Leading-championing the marketplace.
Fulfill tasks, schedules.	Honor-exceed commitments.	Provide value-added.
Live and let live.	Our corner of the world.	The global village.
Learning.	Knowledge.	Wisdom.

Growth Strategies to Succeed in Ever-Changing Times

Businesses cannot exist in a vacuum. They must interact with the outside world, predict the trends, and master front-burner issues affecting the climate and opportunities in which they function. This includes stimulating "outside-the-box" thinking, building customer coalitions, and distinguishing your company from the pack.

There are several good reasons to embrace change management: It beats the alternative. Organizations that and professionals who become stuck in ruts and stubbornly cling to the past are dinosaurs, which the marketplace will pass by.

Professionals, specialists, and technicians owe their careers and livelihoods to change. Because they are educated and experienced at new techniques, they have market power.

Change is not as high-risk as some people fear. Failure to change costs the company six times more. Lost business, opportunity costs, and product failures are signs of neglect, poor management, and failure to plan-anticipate and grow the company.

Those who champion change advance their companies and careers. It accelerates the learning curve and success ratio. Those who do not get on the bandwagon will not last in the company. Those who excel develop leadership skills, empowered teams, and efficiencies.

Change helps you do business in the present and helps plan for the future. Without mastering the challenges of a changing world, companies will not be optimally successful. The organization that manages change remains successful and ahead of the competition, and is a business-industry leader. Meanwhile, other companies will have become victims of change because they stood by and did nothing.

There are many types of businesses in today's global economy. Many factors affect their ability to grow, much less their chances for longevity. The art of business survival lies in distinguishing each tree from the forest, each forest from the environment, and each environment from the global village. Trees may exist or even thrive in one forest (business climate).

Everyone must be measured and champion their own accountability. The natural order is chaos. It requires organization and purpose to create order. The art and skill with which order is achieved equates to growth strategies.

Growth does not necessarily mean bigger. Growth can be lateral—moving a company into ancillary businesses or into new business areas. It will be most successful when it is strategic, planned, measured, and with applications to the next inevitable plateau. Strategy sustains for business crises. Strategy determines growth, along with opportunities, challenges, and methodologies that will address the future, varying with each company. Companies should establish a formal visioning program.

Levels of Standards and Ethics

In order to progress and successfully navigate through the pains, changes, and remedies, every organization has to develop its core values and a corporate culture. Though not a part of the organization's initial phase, having standards and ethics will navigate the journey to success more forceful and surely.

Here are seven progressive levels of standards and ethics, paralleling each category of the Business Tree:

Base Level: Just needing and attempting to get by. Basics of food, clothing, and shelter. Knowing right from wrong. Trying to pursue a good life and aspire to something higher.

Lowest Common Denominators: Although knowing better, subscribing to prevailing philosophies and behaviors of others. This leads some to take advantage of the system, want more than one's share, and fail to be accountable. Sadly, the common denominators are below what they used to be, and society continues to lower them. The mission of a successful person or organization is not to succumb quite that low.

Lessons From the School of Hard Knocks: Learning by experiences, trial and error, successes, and life skills. Becoming more familiar with one's strengths, weaknesses, opportunities, and threats. Understanding what an organization can and cannot accomplish, represent, and become. Maximizing one's resources to the most practical advantage.

Launching a Quest: Striving to learn more and go further. Includes intellectual pursuits, professional realities, nurturing of people skills, and executive abilities. At this point, people change careers, and organizations revisit their goals and crystallize new visions.

Standards: Set and respect boundaries. Many times, people and organizations attempt to violate those standards or fail to acknowledge their existence. The test is how consistently one sets, modifies, and observes one's own standards.

Values and Vision: No person or organization stands still. It is not enough to accept change but more importantly to benefit from it. It is not enough to see yourself on a higher plateau and quest for more. Success comes from charting a course, encompassing value systems, and methodically reaching goals.

Code of Ethics: Fundamental canons, rules of practice, professional obligations, accountability-measurability, professional development, integrity, objectivity, and independence. Commitment to uphold and enforce codes of ethics (yours and those of others) and the ethical responsibilities of members in business.

Taking the Ethical High Road

Corporate responsibility means operating a business in ways that meet or exceed the ethical, legal, commercial, and public expectations that society has of business. This is a comprehensive set of strategies, methodologies, policies, practices, and programs that are integrated throughout business operations, supported, and rewarded by top management.

The growth of corporate responsibility as an issue and a mandate in the "new order of business" stems from several events and trends:

- Changing expectations of stakeholders regarding business.
- Government's reduced role in a deregulated era.
- Increased customer interest and pressure.
- Supply chain responsibility in the age of collaborations, outsourcing, and partnering.
- Growing investor insistence upon accountability.
- Intensively competitive labor markets.
- Voiced concerns by activist organizations.
- Demands for increased communication and disclosure.
- Emerging issues that widen the scope of business.
- Identification of new pockets of stakeholders.

The value of corporate responsibility can be measured in quantitative and qualitative ways. Companies have experienced bottom-line benefits, including improved financial performance, reduced operating costs, access to capital, increased sales and customer loyalty, positive reactions to brand image and reputation, heightened productivity, employee commitments to quality, empowered loyal workforces, and reduced regulatory oversight.

Corporate Social Responsibility is concerned with treating stakeholders of the company ethically or in a socially responsible manner. Consequently, behaving socially responsibly will increase the human development of stakeholders both within and outside the corporation.

Corporate Sustainability aligns an organization's products and services with stakeholder expectations, thereby adding economic, environmental, and social value. This looks at how good companies become better.

Corporate Governance constitutes a balance between economic and social goals and between individual and community goals. The corporate governance framework is there to encourage the efficient use of resources and equally to require accountability for community stewardship of those resources.

Ethical priorities for your company in the "new order of business" may likely be addressed in the event that you:

- Create a corporate code of ethics.

- Create the role of Corporate Ethics Officer.

- Learn to identify issues involved in making corporate ethical decisions.

- Recognize the considerations in the analysis and resolution of ethical dilemmas.

- Apply ethical rules and guidelines toward corporate workplace situations.

- Refine your company's complaint process and investigation procedures.

- Adjudicate employee conduct arising under the corporate Code of Ethics.

- Widen the sensitivity toward issues which may lead toward legal liabilities.

- Embrace standard ethical reporting and compliance procedures.

- Increase the frequency of corporate and personal ethical judgments and decisions.

Great Business and Life Lessons Learned

⇒ Acquire visionary perception.

⇒ Never stop learning, growing, and doing. In short, never stop!

⇒ Offer value-added service. Keep the focus on the customer.

⇒ Lessons from one facet of life are applicable to others.

⇒ Learn from failures, reframing them as opportunities.

⇒ Learn to expect, predict, understand, and relish success.

⇒ Contribute to the big picture of the company and the bottom line, directly and indirectly.

⇒ Prepare for unexpected turns. Benefit from them, rather than becoming victim of them.

⇒ Realize that there are no quick fixes for real problems.

⇒ It is not WHEN you learn, but THAT you learn.

⇒ The path of one's career has dynamic twists and turns, if a person is open to explore them.

⇒ Learn to pace and be in the chosen career for the long run. Behave as a gracious winner.

⇒ Find a truthful blend of perception and reality with emphasis upon substance, rather than style.

⇒ Realize that, as the years go by, one's dues-paying accelerates, rather than decreases.

⇒ Understand what you're good at.

⇒ Be realistic about what you're best at.

⇒ Concentrate on those areas where they intersect.

⇒ There is ALWAYS a next plateau, when we seek it.

⇒ Continue growing as a person and as a professional and quest for more enlightenment.

⇒ Be mentored by others. Act as a mentor to still others.

⇒ One learns to become his/her own best role model.

Value Analysis of a Healthy, Nourished Business

Only at such time as the strategic plan is implemented to assure consistency in purpose, then the following components of a company vision may be expected to ring true, per each category of the Business Tree:

1. **The Business You're In:** Products and services reflect marketplace needs of today and the future. Processes are continually updating themselves. The expansion of your business is a natural outgrowth of carefully planned and well-implemented strategy. You give customers what they cannot really get elsewhere.

   Turn crises, trends, and disappointments into lessons well learned. When we see the downfalls and comebacks of others, we optimize potential in ourselves. Crystallize your niche and scope. Study and refine your own core business characteristics. Make investments toward quality controls.

2. **Running the Business:** Though company leadership influences vision, the process of implementing it must involve the total organization. Operations continue to streamline and are professional and productive. The company's demonstrated integrity and dependability assure customers that the team will perform magnificently.

   Make objective analyses of how the organization has operated to date. Document practices, procedures, operations, and structure in writing. The physical plant is regularly studied, updated, and modified. Distribution standards are documented, practiced, and measured. Time management and "just in time" concepts are applied. Plans are in writing to address inventories and reducing surplus. Outsourcing, privatizing, and collaborating plans are annually updated, with realistic, measurable goals.

   Reduce entrenched fears and defeating characteristics. Use technology wisely. Maintain quality controls that exceed the specifications. Multiply the number of win-win situations.

3. **Financial:** The company has a fiduciary responsibility to run effectively and profitably. All must respect this, though finance cannot govern all aspects of company activity. Keeping the cash register ringing is not the only reason for being in business. You always give customers their money's worth. Your charges are fair and reasonable.

    Cost containment is one (but not the only) factor of company operations. Each product-service is budgeted. Assets are adequately valued and managed. Cash flow, forecasting, and budgeting are consistently monitored.

    Business is run economically and efficiently, with excellent accounting procedures, payables-receivables practices, and cash management. Basing future projections upon past achievements invites unfair expectations. Reduce opportunity costs. Optimize the book value of the company.

4. **People:** No organization lives or dies by one person. The successful company is people-friendly, improving productivity by making higher investments in human capital. Employees know their jobs, are empowered to make decisions, and have high morale in carrying the company banner forward. Every employee must be accountable for his/her activities and is sufficiently trained.

    Collaborations assure that the best talent is assembled. Top management has as a priority the need to develop and practice people-development skills and team-building responsibilities. Management and employees become highly accountable. The employee teams are empowered and competent, and demonstrate initiative and judgment.

    Codes of ethics and corporate responsibility are observed. The corporate culture reflects a formal visioning program.

5. **Business Development:** Strategic planning gives you a better understanding of the marketplace in which your company competes. External factors of the marketplace must always influence the products produced and services rendered.

   Customer input must factor into all long-term planning decisions. Customer service is always the focus. Communications are open, frequent, professional, and with a deep sense of caring.

   All members of top management have business development responsibilities required of them. The company has and regularly fine-tunes a communications strategy. Components include plans for sales, marketing, advertising, public relations, research, and marketplace development, annually updated, with realistic, measurable goals.

6. **Body of Knowledge:** There is a sound understanding of the relationship of each business function to the other. Each part of the organization must learn more about and how to interact better with the others. A condition of departments living in a myopic vacuum is not acceptable to your progressive organization.

   Performance reviews are conducted annually, with realistic, measurable goals. The company learns how to benefit from changes, predicting and staying ahead of trends. Management learns and understands the lessons of failure as the basis for future success. The organization takes a more global view. Everything that goes on outside our company affects our business in some way.

   You provide leadership for progress, rather than following along. Create strategies that previously never existed. Go outside the box more than ever before. Collaborations, partnering, and joint venturing are successful. You develop and champion the tools with which to change.

7. **The Big Picture:** Shared organizational vision is a road map for progressive growth. Things do not just happen without thoughtful planning and strategy. The company leadership approaches business as a lifetime track record of accomplishments.

You maintain and regularly benchmark a strategy for the future, reflecting the society in which we live. In the conduct of business, you ethically walk the talk.

Generating new ideas enables companies to broaden the understanding of what is possible. Sustain a corporate culture that seeks to do right and be our best. Therefore, business becomes more creative, effective, and profitable.

Review the progress. Benchmark the accomplishments, which serves as planning for the next phase. Analyze accomplishments in terms of overall organizational vision and implications for successful achievement of long-term company objectives.

Shared vision is crafted, articulated, and followed. The ongoing emphasis is upon updating, fine-tuning, and improving the corporate culture. The CEO shares strategies and philosophies with employees and stakeholders. Creative business practices are most welcome here.

Strategic planning is viewed as vital to business survival and future success. Outside-the-box thinking does indeed apply to us and will be sought. The organization maintains and lives by an ethics statement. The organization supports change and maintains a change management program.

How Companies Develop Staying Power

Some companies are one-hit wonders, having limited utility, and don't have what it takes to go the distance. They live short lives because that's all they've got in them. Some stay around a little longer than they should have, not because they are doing right things, but because they have just stuck around.

Certain organizations are needed to fulfill particular niches. They don't try to be all things to all people. They have a specialized purpose and make an effort to justify their niche, not just to fill it by default. They take pride in being the best in their area of expertise. Do business with other quality-oriented companies.

Companies with proven products are the most willing to do the planning that is necessary for growth. Products and processes only represent one-third of a company's picture. Growth companies take risks and address the other two-thirds on a regular, systematic basis.

Companies with staying power have earned respect to continue in business. They dare to innovate, with a commitment to improvement. Holistic organizations look outward, viewing their products, processes, and people as a continuum of growth.

Solid companies make contributions beyond the bottom line. They understand other reasons for being in business than just the dollars. They make healthy profits, while creating the best products, being a learning organization, upholding industry standards, and continuing to justify their leadership position.

This book has suggested wide-scope strategies for serving mutual goals, fulfilling mutual responsibilities and the effective use of organizational resources, talents, and expertise.

There are three kinds of approaches to business life (individuals and corporate cultures). *Todayers* are those who do well now and embrace change and growth as viable concepts. *Somedayers* will languish and never realize their potential. *Yesterdayers* will wither and die because they perennially fought change.

Winning teams surrender the "me" for the "we." No company lives nor dies by its CEO alone. Paying outrageous salaries and perks to a CEO does not assure company success, vision, and sustenance. Overpaying a CEO must be a shared blame. Possible consequences always come as a shock.

People who have no goals are destined to work for and be influenced by those who do have worthwhile, well-conceived, and achievable goals. Others have partial information, hidden agendas, and myopic views of reality.

Success is a journey, not a destination. Failure is the end of a trip and the beginning of a bigger, brighter journey. Reaching your destination is one thing. But what follows is what really counts.

Looking holistically at the organization, then down to each part as a contributing factor to the big picture, and again back to the larger scope is my recommendation for running creative, effective, and profitable companies.

Making and Taking Your Company's Future

Alas, the big picture is an ongoing process of re-examining the small pieces, redefining each business function, and growing concepts of the business itself.

Vision + caring + commitment + implementation + follow-through = a successful company.

If any of the elements are missing, the equation does not add up. An incomplete equation means that a company will falter and fail.

Perspective is the most changeable part of doing business. Understand from where you came, and it will indicate where you may be headed. Spend more time analyzing it. That is where solutions for problems present themselves. Through deep insight into your perspective comes the route toward success. Without perspective, you never make the journey. No quick fix on earth will make the journey for you.

Good companies sandbag themselves by doing nothing. Doing anything—even making a few mistakes—is better than doing nothing. I've spent more than 40 years of my career trying to explain that concept to otherwise-reasonable people who simply stick their heads in the sand.

Truisms of Careers and Business Success

→ Whatever measure you give will be the measure that you get back.

→ The joy is in the journey, not in the final destination.

→ The best destinations evolve out of circumstances.

→ Circumstances can be managed, for maximum effectiveness.

→ You gotta give to get.

→ Getting and having are not the same thing.

→ As an integrated process of life skills, career has its place.

→ A body of work is the culmination of a thoughtful, dedicated process, from some point forward.

→ The objective is to begin that strategizing point sooner rather than later.

Sustaining the 7 Most Important Business Mindsets

1. Steady, Managed Growth. Look to craft innovative strategies.

2. Product and Process Realignment. Collaborations build sustainable communities.

3. Human Intelligence. You are in the credibility business.

4. Professional development, ethics, values, accountability, and the public opinion all matter.

5. Body of Knowledge. Representing business is honorable, laudable, and challenging.

6. The Big Picture. Careful nurturing of your Business Tree yields results.

7. Don't forget to think, plan, dream, and team.

Read and learn from case studies of failure and success. Understand why decisions were made, the conditions affecting them, and the ramifications of actions and non-actions. Think the way the boss and the workers do. Learn to see company activities from every possible perspective.

Research and stay current on front-burner issues affecting the climate and opportunities in which key corporate executives function. Stimulate outside-the-box thinking. Build customer coalitions. Distinguish your company from the pack.

The old ways of doing business will not cut it in the future. Every organization must look forward in order to survive and succeed. The skill with which one adapts-changes makes the difference between the company simply existing and moving forward in a growth mode.

The manner in which one navigates through the rocky times and takes proactive steps to recovering from inevitable setbacks speaks toward long-term success. Taking shortcuts will actually deter the journey toward success.

Collaborations with other people create success. One cannot be successful alone or working in a vacuum. One is always dependent upon other people, and other people are dependent upon you. Commitments must be made to other people.

One must view the future and change as affirmative, in order to succeed. Knowledge of results is a powerful force in growing and learning.

By establishing new ways of working together, we paint new horizons for organizational success, individually and collectively. When we take creative approaches toward problem-solving, dealing with business realities, and strategic planning, we assure that organizations will truly succeed.

We must learn from the mistakes of our own companies and those of others in order to create a more successful business. Without this learning curve, we are destined to make more mistakes and derail the success that the organization has earned. Know how you can be wrong. Learning more information and new approaches leads to success. There is nothing more "right" than a newly enlightened perspective.

Learn the trends and how to live in between them. By spotting trends beyond the obvious ones we might not otherwise have considered, we take creative steps and assure a better ruin of business success.

Changes are typified by multiple factors—not by one. Assess the judgment of decision-makers. Analyze the significance and probabilities of developments. Know where to draw the line between what can be done and what is impossible. Keep developing your quest to do something meaningful, and do it very well.

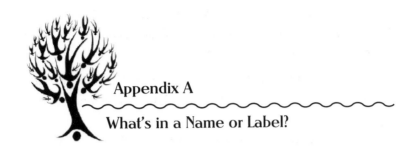

Appendix A

What's in a Name or Label?

People and companies make decisions based upon partial business models and the wrong information all the time. There is no reason why they cannot make new decisions based upon a widened scope of business, a fresh set of eyes, and the desire to acquire new information.

The genesis of this piece started with two influential school teachers. My junior high school speech teacher, Thelma Henslee, used to quiz us with the phrase "Author or Arthur?" Her point was to discern sound-alike expressions and think through their differences, similarities, correct usage, and applicability.

My high school speech teacher, Terri Flynn, used to ask people, "How are you doing?" The typical response was "Real good." She would then probe, "How good?" She wanted you to use correct grammar, such as "really well." More importantly, she wanted you to choose less-trite expressions, such as "outstandingly fine today" or, more honestly, how you really were doing or thinking.

From those teachers and subsequent professional mentors, I learned the value of:

- Using specific, imaginative language to express ideas.

- Saying what you mean and meaning what you say.

- Calling the elephant what it really is.

- Writing for the eye. It's different from writing for the ear.

- Not settling for trite expressions, slang jargon, and other people's quotes.

- Taking the time to educate people on subtle nuances and meanings of words.

- Believing that listeners and readers are more intelligent than others might believe.

- Using vocabulary that expresses thoughts and rises to higher levels.

- Challenging people to read new meanings into old words, phrases, and ideas.

- Compelling people to discern ideas for themselves, based upon insights and ideas.

In business (a mirror of everyday life), terms are used interchangeably and out of context. The public doesn't discern differences. With the passage of time, as people and companies "market the hype," they begin to believe the blurred usages of expressions they use.

Thus, improper semantics perpetuate in the mass culture. Constituents accept what they hear. If they hear it enough times, it must be true. They believe what they are familiar with. Getting them to modify familiar patterns is difficult but still must be done.

Cases in point:

Retailers offer "service" as an enticer to close sales of products. Sales support and follow-up customer service are light years away. Whereas they'll say anything to make a sale, true-quality customer service is presently at an all-time low. There are many tiers of service, with service to make the sale merely the lowest rung on the ladder.

Business "consultants" often misrepresent what they do. Accounting firms believe themselves to be full-scope business advisors and sell themselves as such. Training companies tell clients that they also conduct strategic planning and consulting, believing all of those professional disciplines are the same thing.

There are many differences in business. Sales and marketing are not the same thing. Advertising and public relations are different services. Financial projections do not constitute business planning. Sales quotas do not produce an empowered staff. Edicts by management do not directly lead to behavioral modification. Selling more products does not solve the manufacturing and distribution problems. Career workers and seasoned professionals are different breeds. Grumbling by workers does not constitute discontent and mutiny.

People place labels on everything and everybody, without distinguishing the subtle differences. People and companies believe the labels, without looking into the subtle nuances. Society was not acclimated into discerning differences.

All differences become opportunities to educate each other about the subtle nuances of labels, terms, phrases, and categories.

Judge for Yourself the Relationship of Terms in Each Set to the Other

Sales—Service

Medicine—Healthcare

Fame—Fortune

Business—Finance

Law—Order

Wealth—Riches

Learning—Knowledge

Banking—Finance

Pencil—Pen

Expert—Expertise

Government—
  Bureaucracy

Worker—Laborer

Career—Profession

Sales—Marketing
Ideas—Ideologies
Chairman—President
Rights—Privileges
Car—Truck
Technology—Equipment
Hearing—Listening
Oil—Water
Management—Labor
Breakfast—Brunch
Audio—Video
Advertising—Public Relations
Culture—Class
Street—Road
Avenue—Boulevard
Health—Wellness
Consult—Advise
Bookkeeping—Accounting
Science—Technology
Own—Rent
Lease—Buy
Concepts—Philosophies
Cassette—CD
Knowledge—Wisdom
Words—Grammar
Today—This Day
History—The Past
Sunlight—Moonlight
Comfort—Ease

Ignorance—Stupidity
Caring—Convictions
Parts—Labor
Air Conditioner—Fan
Education—Training
Lake—Bay
Thinker—Conceptor
Watcher—Doer
Parts—Whole
Champagne—Wine
Trade—Skill
Art—Science
Empathy—Sympathy
Planning—Execution
Goals—Tactics
Researching—Benchmarking
Mission—Vision
Food—Groceries
Violator—Perpetrator
Advertising—Promotion
Before—After
Advocate—Activist
Teaching—Learning
Fun—Games
Closets—Storage
Honest—Truthful
Start—Embark
The FBI—The CIA
Barber—Hair Stylist

Allow—Enable

Insurance—Assurance

Ethnic—Multicultural

Bake—Broil

Driver—Chauffeur

Bus—Trolley

Cook—Chef

Athlete—Sportsman

Explain—Convey

Lies—Deceptions

Confidence—Self-Esteem

Need—Want

Sip—Gulp

Compliance—Agreement

Couch—Loveseat

Drink—Slurp

Business—Marketplace

Garden—Forest

Read—Absorb

Non-Smoker—Ex-Smoker

Wealthy—Rich

Try—Attempt

Award—Reward

Problem—Dilemma

Brief—Short

Terminal—Hangar

Prisoner—Hostage

Time—Space

Manager—Leader

Progress—Progression

Resolve—Solve

Dinner—Supper

Genetics—Heredity

See—View

Believe—Perceive

Weather—Environment

Picture—Photo

Police—Highway Patrol

Fiction—Nonfiction

Peace—Calm

News—Entertainment

Carport—Garage

Van—Bus

Thinking—Intuiting

Multiply—Divide

Book—Novel

Store—Dealer

Birthday—Anniversary

Cow—Bull

Misunderstanding—
Disagreement

Mailing—Shipping

Legend—Icon

Grocery Shopping—
Marketing

Product Selling—Marketing

Seeing—Believing

Collaboration—
Cooperation

Research—Development

Jumbo—Shrimp

Lighting—Illumination

Advise—Consent

Music—Lyrics

Crime—Criminal Justice

Clinic—Hospital

Gun—Rifle

Diplomat—Ambassador

Speaking—Talking

Look—See

Misstatement—Un-Truth

Study—Investigate

Right—Correct

Volunteerism—Stewardship

Competent—Proficient

Rain—Humidity

Tollway—Turnpike

Potential—Likely

Tire—Wheel

Business Trip—Vacation

Tablets—Caplets

Illness—Disease

Film—Slide Show

Teacher—Mentor

Time—Motion

Space—Cyberspace

Gasoline—Petroleum

Think—Believe

Habit—Fixation

Warranty—Guarantee

Deny—Disallow

Heredity—Environment

Child Care—Day Care

Sense—Fear

Upstream—Downstream

Friend—Supporter

Respect—Trust

Write-Down—Bad Debt

Payables—Receivables

Credit—Debit

Baseball—Softball

Reading—Literacy

Restaurant—Cafe

Sickness—Disability

Friends—Associates

Movie—Cinema

Neglect—Dysfunction

Detergent—Clean Laundry

Words—Ideas

Learning—Common Sense

Futurism—Evolution

Mental—Physical

Dependable—Reliable

Ratio—Proportion

Reward—Punish

Grocery Store—Supermarket

Package—Container

Bottle—Jar

Instructor—Professor

Arts—Entertainment

Process—System

Coordinate—Expedite

Booklet—Brochure

House—Home

Overpass—Bridge

Language—Grammar

Sauce—Gravy

Decisions—Consequences

Police—Sheriff

Test—Quiz

Corp. Culture—Employee Attitude

Ideas—Innovations

Rain—Rainbows

Confidence—Arrogance

Plate—Platter

Cool—Cold

Desire—Covet

Separate—Distinctive

Warm—Hot

Mad—Angry

Trivet—Potholder

Buy—Sell

Dawn—Daybreak

Rain—Drizzle

Cup—Mug

Hobby—Avocation

TV Set—Monitor

Oil—Energy

Instinct—Behavior

Hills—Mountains

Pamphlet—Guide

Collaborate—Cooperate

Business—Commerce

Request—Demand

Analysis—Assessment

Flowers—Plants

Mind—Behave

Picture—Painting

Trees—Bushes

Box—Container

Reporter—Correspondent

Height—Stature

Sack—Bag

Dead-End Street—Cul de Sac

Community—Society

City—Town

Private Sector—Business

Safety—Protection

Solids—Liquids

Public Sector—Government

Probable—Possible

Noise—Sounds

Witness—Observer

Soap—Shampoo

Light—Lamp

Violin—Fiddle

River—Stream

Pets—Strays

Briefcase—Satchel

Hero—Martyr

File—Folder

Scene—Scenario

Consciousness—Awareness

Battle—War

Diagnose—Prescribe

Grass—Weeds

Group—Team

Symptoms—Problems

Stress—Pressure

Cause—Effect

Pleasure—Pain

Originator—Follower

Pan—Skillet

Thrills—Excitement

Create—Initiate

Report—Memo

Socks—Stockings

Diamond—Jewel

Medicine—Pills

Earnings—Annual Report

Floor—Ground

Letter—Note

Facilitator—Implementer

Employee—Colleague

Contender—Winner

Rebate—Discount

Bookshelf—Bookcase

Horn—Siren

Refund—Make Good

Remember—Reflect

Live—Exist

Sugar—Sweetener

Manage—Control

Give—Receive

Alarm—Frighten

Order—Empower

Show—Play

Eating—Dining

Earn—Receive

Opera—Operetta

Theater—Auditorium

Adjudicate—Solve

Fan—Supporter

Consulting—Visioning

Newsletter—Direct Mail

Groupie—Star

Training—Planning

Taxi—Limousine

Jail—Prison

IRS—Treasury Dept.

Resident—Citizen

Coffee—Tea

Eyesight—Vision

Doctor—Nurse

Bath—Shower

Financial Planning—Banking

Lawyer—Paralegal

Store—Shop

Advise—Supervise

MD—PhD—EdD

Ice Cream—Yogurt

Sales Goals—Business Plan

Compliant—Obedient

Furnace—Stove

Heart Attack—Stroke

Library—The Internet

Delete—Destroy

Notebook—Reference File

Wastebasket—Trash Can

Message—Medium

Loudspeaker—Sound System

Limitations—Realities

Catalog—Brochure

Screaming—Discussing

Tastes—Preferences

Hotel—Mot

Change—Resistance

Flavors—Fragrances

Smile—Enthusiasm

Telephone Etiquette—Manners

Capitalism—Opportunism

Mystery—Suspense

Spokesperson—Decision-Maker

Expense—Investment

Account—Compute

Human Resources—Leadership

Differences—Barriers

Think—Feel

Professional—Vendor

Associate—Hanger-On

Dial—Knob

Obvious—Subtle

Interpret—Modify

Stop—Cease

Roles—Responsibilities

Priorities—Agendas

Start—Commence

Entrepreneur—Employee

Mini-Series—Soap Opera

Boss—Staff

Plant—Equipment

Seasoning—Experiences

Attitude—Success

Labels—Mindset

Improvement—Results

Wheels—Motion

Telephone Solicitor—
Nuisance

Healthy Lifestyle—Longevity

Diameter—Circle

Planning—Achieving

Review—Future Planning

Facts—Figures

Forms—Processes

Experiences—
Philosophies

Shirt—Sweater

Lack of Planning—Failure

Ethics—Responsibility

Chair—Stool

Cash Flow—Market Trends

Insurance Premiums—Claims

Research—Planning

Company Brochure—
Performance

Company History—Future
Plan

Youth—Mistakes

Transportation—Distribution

Discipline—Work Ethics

Flash—Sizzle

Inputting—Database
Accuracy

Discipline—Behaviors

Quality—Success

Appendix B

The Organization Tree: 7 Major Parts-Components of an Individual's Life Experiences

Organizations are populated with individuals who possess a plethora of education, skills, and talents. Companies are comprised of human beings, who bring their cultural backgrounds and experiences to the job. Thus, they set the pace for the tree (company) in question.

Business professionals are the sum of their life experiences. People, as do organizations, develop, grow, and thrive. If not, they are of little market value in a career.

Any individual is like a tree. He/she seemingly looks the same each day but sheds leaves, lets its limbs rot, and applies band-aid surgery to the branches late in life. Therefore, that person's career does not fully grow and bloom.

If properly nourished, the growth process is steady and consistent. Many people neglect themselves and thus fail to reach full potential. If the individual stoops to the declining mode, his/her career will wane and fail to exist.

People do not look the same, but they have common cultural needs. Like organizations, people trees possess qualities that are relative to the environment in which they attempt to grow. Without proper care, they wither. Without continued care, they die. With proper care, they blossom. With continued care, they sprout deep roots and live a richer life.

The Organization Tree has seven major parts: five branches, a trunk (6), and the base (7). Like organizations, most people address only three or four categories at any given time—some effectively and others not.

No single branch (life component) constitutes a healthy tree. None of the limbs, twigs, and leaves on each branch provide all the nourishment required to breed a healthy tree (person). Each branch has its proper responsibility and should learn to interface with the others.

The Organization Tree will not stand without a trunk and the base. These keep the branches, limbs, twigs, and leaves on a growth curve. Trees with thicker bases and deeper roots will sprout greener (be happy-productive), shed less often (fewer career mistakes), and live longer (create and sustain a body of work).

These components of the Organization Tree parallel those on the Business Tree:

1. Life.
   - Environment, family.
   - Meeting physical needs.
   - Food, water, clothing, shelter.
   - Knowing how to get by.
   - Rules and regulations.
   - Acceptable and unacceptable behaviors.
   - Street-wise attributes.
   - Safety and preparedness.
   - Interfacing with others who know.
2. Living Well.
   - Personal management.
   - Home administration, upkeep.
   - Health and wellness.

- Meeting social needs.
- Entertainment.
- Behavior.
- Communication skills.
- Subtleties and niceties of life.
- Fine wine (the process of living well).

3. Working Well.
   - Economic survival.
   - Fiduciary responsibilities.
   - Meeting needs to create, achieve, and excel.
   - Talents and skills.
   - Professional orientation, demeanor.
   - Time, skills, and energy management.
   - Training, organizational development.
   - Areas of expertise.
   - Change management.

4. Education.
   - Meeting intellectual needs.
   - Multiple interests.
   - Formal schooling.
   - Technical training.
   - Professional development.
   - Literacy skills enhancement.
   - Arts appreciation, support.
   - Non-credit learning for fun.
   - Hobbies.

5. Philosophy.
   - Viewpoint (senses/mind connected together).
   - Inspiration.
   - Meeting spiritual, moral, ethical needs.

- Common sense.
- Maintain focus and perspective.
- Committed to amassing knowledge, insight.
- Perceptions and realities.
- Adaptabilities, flexibilities.

6. Self-Fulfillment.
   - Meeting emotional needs.
   - Psychological enhancement.
   - Comfort from within.
   - Interpersonal relationship building.
   - Self-growth.
   - Trust, caring, sharing, tenderness, empathy, sensitivity.
   - Thinking and feeling concepts.
   - Seeks-fulfills balance in life.
   - Learning from failure and success.
   - Balancing needs and wants.
   - Aged cheese (sharpening-amassing of life skills).

7. Purpose and Commitment.
   - Goals for life.
   - Community stewardship.
   - Continuous quality improvement.
   - Going the distance, getting better.
   - Valuable antiques (accomplishments in life).

Our value to organizations, employees, customers, influential constituencies, and ascendancy to management is a direct reflection of mastering the life skills listed on the Organization Tree.

A professional must examine the context in which they work, pursue a career, and operate their business. To be valued as professionals, we must continually enrich ourselves, covering all five major branches of the tree, plus the trunk and base.

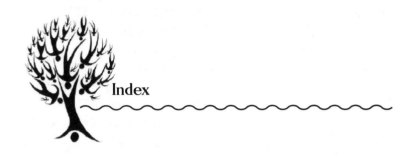

Index

# About the Author

Hank Moore is a business advisor, speaker, and author. He is a Corporate Strategist™, with original, cutting-edge ideas for creating, implementing, and sustaining corporate growth throughout every sector of the organization. He conducts business appraisals, evaluations, and strategic planning and company visioning.

He developed four trademarked concepts of business, heralded widely for ways to remediate corporate damage, enhance productivity, and facilitate better business. He discusses topics from having advised them over a long career:

- Business trends, challenges, and opportunities.
- Corporate responsibility and ethics.
- Creating and rebuilding corporate cultures.
- New ways of doing business in the future.
- Visioning and strategic planning.
- Building coalitions, collaborations, and joint ventures.
- Crisis management and preparedness.

Hank Moore has spoken at five economic summits and spoke at think tanks for five U.S. presidents. He has provided senior-level advising services for more than 5,000 client organizations (including 100 of the Fortune 500), companies in transition (startup, re-engineering, mergers, going public), public sector entities, professional associations, and non-profit organizations. He has worked with all major industries throughout a 40-year career.

He is an expert on big picture issues and how core business specialists may enlarge their scope and assume mantles of greater responsibility and recognition. Mr. Moore has overseen strategic plans and corporate visioning processes. He has conducted performance reviews of organizations. He is a mentor to senior management and advises at the executive committee and board levels, providing big picture ideas.

Hank Moore speaks and advises companies about growth strategies, visioning, planning, executive-leadership development, futurism, and the issues that profoundly affect the business climate. The Business Tree™ is his trademarked approach to growing, strengthening, and evolving business, while mastering change. In 2002, business visionary Peter Drucker termed Hank Moore's Business Tree as the most original business model of the past 40 years.

Types of speaking engagements that Hank Moore presents include:

- Conference opening keynote.
- Corporate planning retreats.
- Ethics and corporate responsibility speeches.
- University and college commencement addresses.
- Business think tanks.
- International business conferences.
- Non-profit and public sector planning retreats.

Additional materials may be found on Hank Moore's Website (*www.hankmoore.com*).